"THE MURDER POLICE"

Inspired from Real Case Files from Chicago's

Detective Division

The Case Of: Gregory Allen & Roger Keith

"Murders of Seven People in Five Months"

By Retired Sergeant: Judge Hardy

~Dedication~

*To the Chicago Police Department and the elite Homicide Unit
of detectives that only handles murders referred to as...*

"The Murder Police"

~*Introduction*~

On October 14, 2003, the citizens of Chicago were glued to their television sets watching the Cub's play the Florida Marlins in game five of the national league playoffs. Simultaneously, on the far south side of the city, two young struggling drug addicted women entered into an abandoned house for the purpose of having sex for drugs unaware that they would never leave again. The two men whom they met will go on a killing spree over the next few months killing others before the police become aware of their crimes. It is now a race between killers who are now planning to kill again, and

"The Murder Police" who must stop them before two more innocent women are murdered. The language is transparent and the people are real. This story is authentic and it leaves you on the very edge of your seat with a racing spell bounded heart until its end. This is one of many tragic true cases of Chicago's finest...

"The Murder Police"

~Acknowledgments~

To begin with, I could have not written this book without the support of my wonderful wife Janice. From day one, she encouraged me emotionally and spiritually throughout the writing process. I would also like to express my gratitude to my editor, Ms. Valerie Allen of VJ Publishing House for her countless hours of revising, proofing, and guidance. With gratefulness and love, I extend a great big thank-you to the members of the Chicago Police Department, and to the elite group of men and women of Area 2 that were assigned before I got there, and to the ones that are currently there today. Words cannot express my indebtedness to have been afforded the opportunity to work with so many great police officers in Area 2. I want to give a very special thanks to investigator Johnnie Robinson. In 1978, I was granted the opportunity to work with Mr. Robinson my very first day on the job in Area

2. Although I was considered too young (twenty-seven years

old) with only five years on the job (inexperienced), he saw

something in me that other's didn't see. He took me under his

wings and pushed me until I was ready to work in the Youth

Division. In the years that followed, my life would forever

change because of his wisdom, ability and leadership skills.

Through his fatherly advice, along with his keen sense of

understanding that young black lives really matter, before the

"Black Lives Matter" movement was ever born. His greatest

attribute was his knowledge and the way he showed respect

for all people. Through his mentoring, I was able to change

the mindset of those who once criticized me. These same

powers would later come to admire my work and offer out

praise for my dedication for helping the under-privileged kids

in Area 2. Lastly, with love, honor, and respect, I acknowledge my deceased Father, Judge Hardy Sr. and my Ninety-two year-old Mother, Leola Hardy, who gave me and my brother and five sisters the best childhood a child could ask for growing up on the south side of Chicago. However, the greatest gift of all they bestowed upon us was the ability to know and love God. Thank you Mom and Dad, and most of all God for all that you have done, and doing in my life.

THE MURDER POLICE

~Chapter 1~

As those who grow up in Chicago know, every year, the Cubs and the White Sox donate tickets to the Boy Scouts of America. This is how a lot of kids are able to see their first professional baseball game. You can see groups of them looking and acting as if going to baseball games and having a great time is their regular routine. During baseball season, it's like every kid has a glove and a cap with the team's logo on it. Some kids even have jerseys with their favorite player's name on the back. You can even see whole families wearing some sort of baseball paraphernalia. It also seems like every kid has a baseball program with the names and numbers of every player on both teams. There are a number of fans who bring their gloves to the game in hopes of catching a foul or fair ball; they just want to catch one.

This was especially true on October 14, 2003, when the entire population of the city of Chicago was glued to their televisions as they watched game five of the National League playoff series between the Chicago Cubs and the Florida Marlins. It seemed like every police officer, whether on the streets or in the station house, was watching the game. The same could be said about the Chicago Fire Department—they too were all glued to TV sets. This was no ordinary game. The Chicago Cubs were one win away from the World Series. The last time the Cubs had won a World Series was in 1908. The countdown had begun: five more outs, and the team would be in the World Series.

In what seemed like a world apart—though in reality it was less than twenty-five miles away—sat an old, rundown house located on 109th near Eggleston, in the heart of the Roseland Community. This was one of the last remnants of what had been a thriving middle-class community. The house had been boarded up for years. It had once been used as a shooting gallery for hard drugs, but now it was a crack house. There were no lights or running water. The floors were covered with empty beer and wine bottles, used condoms, and empty vials that had once held crack. In what had once been the living room sat a large cable spool that had been used to hold cable wire. Being used as a cocktail table, it's now a place to sit your drugs and your pipes. There was just enough room to sit a bottle of alcohol and a few cups to share your drink. There were eight empty plastic milk crates turned upside down, each one strategically placed around the spool that served as chairs for entertaining. The large candle that sat in the middle of the makeshift table brought a little light into the room.

This had once been a beautiful two-story, three-bedroom home. If the original owners could have seen their house now, they would have dropped dead at the sight of what it had become. Their piece of the American Dream was now a crack house. All three bedrooms were located on the second floor. This had once been a place where dreams of better things had filled the hallways. Now they were filled with the stale smell of crack cocaine and the pungent odors of urine and feces. The original owners, along with their three children, had left this house filled with some of their fondest memories. They'd celebrated holidays, birthdays, anniversaries, or just coming together to share some great family time in this once lovely home.

The house had a wonderful, spacious basement, the type of basement that during those years, men of Chicago would have called their man-cave. It even had a sign as you entered the basement that read "Da Bears." This was the place the men of the family would gather to watch Bears, Sox, and sometimes even Cubs games while having a beer. It was now pitch black, because all of the windows were boarded up, blocking any chance of light into this former shrine of Chicago sports. Still, there, in the far corner of the basement, was the coal bin, once used to store coal for the cold winter nights in Chicago.

Right around the time Cubs outfielder Moises Alou was moving into position to catch what he believed to be a catchable ball, on the other side of town, two young, once-promising black women, Sandra Nelson, twenty-six, and Kelly Starks, twenty-seven years old, unknowingly walked into this house for the very last time. The two women had become best friends over the past two years, and they had come to know this house so well over the last six months that it felt like home away from home. Sandra and Kelly had not only met men at this house, but they had also taken a number of men to the house. They used the house to get high at times and have sex with different guys. While Cub fans were arguing as to whether it had been fan interference, or a playable ball, the TV cameras continued to replay what Cubs fans could not believe. Not knowing what was to come next, Sandra and Kelly's future also had not yet been decided. Just like the Cubs game, there was a lot still to happen before the night ended.

Earlier that day, Sandra had called her best friend Kelly to tell her that she had met two guys that she had gone to school with. She'd come in contact with them while grocery shopping at Jewel's Food Store near 115th and Halsted. They had exchanged numbers in hopes they could get together later that day. Sandy had told them she would not be free until after six pm because her younger brother was home from school sick. They promised to call her later around that time.

"What do they want to do?" Kelly asked. Known for being impatient, she just wanted to get straight to the point.

"They want to do what we do, and you know how we do it," replied Sandra.

"So they want to get high and party, right?"

"Yep, replied Sandra.

"They got some money?"

"The one guy, Allen, said they just got paid."

"What kind of work do they do?" asked Kelly.

"I did not go into all of that in the middle of the store, girl. Stop asking so many damn questions... You can ask him yourself later tonight. You down, or what, Kelly?"

"I just want to make one thing clear before they get us high. I will suck his dick, but if they want to fuck, they will have to pay me."

"Okay! I'm with you on that," said Sandra.

Around six pm, Sandra received a phone call from a number she did not recognize, but because she had given her cell phone number to several guys, she answered it. It was her classmate Allen from earlier in the day. Sandra wanted to know if this was his cell phone number. He told her no, that he was calling from a payphone because his cell phone battery had gone dead. Because Allen didn't know how the night would end, the last thing he wanted if the police got involved was his cell phone number showing up in her phone.

Right off the bat, Allen asked, "Are you and your friend ready to party?"

Sandra replied, "Damn right we are!"

"Okay, where do I pick you ladies up?"

"How about the gas station at 107th and Halsted?"

"What time?" asked Allen.

"We'll be there in, let's say, about forty-five minutes."

Sandra did not want men coming to her house. She'd had some bad experiences with guys she had done drugs with coming over in the middle of the night, waking up everyone in the house. On one occasion, a guy she'd gotten high with had showed up at her door at three am in the morning, ringing the doorbell like a damn fool. Sandra's father had been forced to call the police because the man refused to leave their porch until Sandra came out. When the police arrived, the man explained that he had paid Sandra for sex in advance and now she was refusing to deliver. The police escorted the man away from the house, but not before embarrassing her in front of her family with all kind of questions clearly designed to make her parents aware of her drug problems. The officers, while giving her and her parents a patronizing look, had suggested she find a more conventional and legal line of work.

Her parents were already aware of her drug problems. They had learned over the last two years how bad it was. It first started with little things coming up missing from the house. Then, one day, the family's TV was gone, right out of their living room. She and her then boyfriend, Roy Bins, staged a break-in of their garage, stealing her father's lawn mower. The two of them started breaking into garages up and down her block. Their addiction eventually grew, and soon they were breaking into her neighbors' homes when the owners were away. Roy was caught breaking into her next-door neighbor's house while Sandra acted as the look out. When the police arrived, she simply and nonchalantly walked back into her house, leaving the boyfriend to take the full rap. Roy was sentenced to five years in prison because this was not his first offense. He never told the police or the courts about Sandra's involvement.

At six thirty pm, Sandra walked the two blocks from her house to the gas station. She was there waiting on Allen when the 1995 white Lexus LX 450 pulled into the gas station. Upon letting the window down, Sandra immediately recognized Allen, who was driving. She remembered his million-dollar smile from high school. It was what attracted her to him, along with his beautiful, smooth brown skin. He was tall and thin, but not skinny. He had broad shoulders to go along with those mesmerizing green eyes. He reminded her of a young Smokey Robinson.

As Allen pulled into the gas station, Keith was already

sitting in the backseat. He rolled down the back window and asked, "What happened to your girlfriend?"

Sandra replied, "She is waiting for us at the liquor store near 111th and Halsted."

Allen smiled and said, "I get it; you ladies want something to drink to help get the party started."

As Sandra seated herself next to Allen in the front seat, she commented on what a nice car he had. Driving south on Halsted, five minutes later, he pulled up in front of the liquor store. When he parked the car, Sandra pointed out her friend, who was standing in front of the store. "That's Kelly!"

Kelly walked over to the car, Keith quickly opened the back door, and the introductions were made. Allen exited the vehicle and then turned around and asked, "Ladies, what would you like to drink?"

"I want some Hennessy," Kelly responded. "We call it 'Hen' because it makes me want to sin! How about you, Sandra?"

"I like 'Hen' too, because I like to drink it while I sin!" The ladies laughed hysterically. "Hey, Allen, don't forget to get some ice and four cups." Turning around, Sandra looked at

Keith and asked him, "So, you don't remember me from high school?"

Keith looked closer at her and, not wanting to hurt her feelings or miss out on the possibility of having sex, said, "You look great. I never would have recognized you after all these years. You look better now than you did back in high school."

Kelly looked over at Keith and asked, "So what is it you guys do for a living?"

Keith smiled and answered, "A little bit of this and a little bit of that."

Both Sandra and Kelly smiled and said, "I feel you."

Of course, this was a lie, one that he and Allen had rehearsed over the past two months. In fact, Allen and Keith had been released from prison just a little over month ago after having served eight years for sexual assault. Prior to their convictions, the both of them had begun following single women home as they left nightclubs after having too much to drink or were high from drugs.

Allen was a good-looking man. With most women, he would wait until he thought they'd had too much to drink, and then he would come on to them. He would ask them questions like: Are you single? Do you have a man in your life? Do you have kids? He would then disappear or walk away, as if he did not like their answers. Sometimes they would follow the women home just to see where they lived and if they lived alone or had kids or a man living with them. They would sometime watch them for months before breaking in on them late at night. They would wear stockings over their faces so they couldn't be easily identified.

This went on for a little over a year until, one night, the two men broke into the apartment of a woman who lived next door to a police officer, who overheard the attack and called for backup. Both men were arrested and charged with seven counts of sexual assault. At the last minute, they both agreed to take a plea deal for fifteen years. They were out in eight, but swore they would never return to jail at any cost.

~Chapter 2~

Though Allen always seemed to be under control, deep down inside he was an angry and disturbed young man who resented his mother. His resentment was due to the type of men she had in her life. It was not unusual for men to leave his mother's bedroom after she had passed out or fallen asleep after having had too much to drink or overdoing it with her drug of choice. These men would often wander into Allen's bedroom and try to have sex with him. He complained to her about them, but she never believed him until, one night, she witnessed one of her boyfriends trying to force himself on Allen. That night, Allen ended up stabbing the man twenty-seven times. The man lived but would never walk again. Allen always wondered what kind of woman was so desperate for a man that she would have loud, raucous sex in the bedroom next to her young son. There were many nights he would hear their conversations as clear as if he were in the room. He often pictured in his mind what was going on just a few feet away, and it made him feel really sad that she gave them more attention than him.

Keith's life was slightly different. His mother had left

him when he was very young, around the tender age of eight years old, due to her drug addiction. He'd been placed in numerous foster homes, where he'd had to fight off would-be abusers. A number of his foster parents had been child abusers, both physical and sexual. He had only seen his real mother once since she'd given him up more than ten years ago. When he did finally see her, she was getting into a car with a man she was going to turn a trick with.

On one occasion, Allen, hanging out with Keith, watched Keith's mother go down on one of her tricks and then engage in full-blown sex in the back seat of his car. When the man finished, he threw a few dollars in her direction like she was a piece of trash. She complained that this was not what they'd agreed upon. The man laughed out loud, spit towards her, and drove off. Looking in her son's direction, she acted as if she didn't know who he was and walked away from both him and Allen without saying a word. Allen spent the rest of the day trying to console his friend. They'd both been freshman in high school at the time it happened. On that night, Allen took Keith home with him, where he lived until they were sent to prison.

Once they served their time and were released, they went

on a spree, doing a number of home burglaries and a couple of armed robberies. They also hijacked or stole cars, including the one they were driving now. They rocked the streets with the stolen white Lexus as if they were ballers.

Standing in line, impatiently waiting to buy the Hennessy, Allen noticed how slowly it was moving. As he got closer to the cashier, he could see the problem. She was watching the Cubs game and a replay of the moment that would change the momentum of the entire game. The Cubs were now down by five runs with one inning left to play.

When Allen got back to the car, Kelly asked him, "Where are we going to get high? Sandra and I like to go to a place we call 'The Den.'" With a bemused look on her face, she asked, "What motel are you guys taking us to if we're not going there?"

"Listen, ladies," said Allen. "I just spent forty-five dollars on a bottle of Hennessy and fifty on some rocks, leaving me with only a few dollars for the both of you. I tell you what; the next time we get together, I promise we will go to a motel, okay?"

"Sure," said Kelly. "However, let me warn you that there

might be some people already there getting high."

Lifting his shirt, Keith revealed his .45-caliber Glock. "But I'll get rid of them fools. I promise you they won't come back there tonight."

It was a short ride from the liquor store to 109th near Eggleston, maybe ten minutes at the most. Arriving, they saw several people walking out of the house. Keith walked over to the group and warned them not to come back, that this was a private party, and he lifted his shirt, revealing his Glock, to get his point across. Allen, along with the ladies, went into the house through the basement door, which at first glance looked to be boarded up. Once inside, the ladies guided them to what was once the living room.

Allen looked around and said, "It's too damn dark in here. I can't see a damn thing." He then told them to hold on a minute so he could retrieve the gas lamp in the trunk of his car. He had discovered the lamp while searching the trunk for anything of value he might be able to sell later. He returned with the lamp, and it was enough light to dimly illuminate the room. Everyone took a seat on one of the plastic milk crates turned upside down. They all sat around a large spool turned on

16

its side that had once been used to hold cable wire. Now it acted as a cocktail table. Allen broke out the cups while asking the girls if they wanted one or two cubes of ice. Both, at the same time, said, "Two cubes, please." Placing the cubes into all four cups, he proceeded to pour the "Hen" until each cup was half-full.

Kelly then asked, "Who got the rocks?"

"I do," said Keith.

"Well, let's get this party started," said Kelly, who was always ready for whatever.

As Keith produced several rocks, Allen pulled out two pipes and handed one over to Kelly.

"Who got the fire?" she said.

With a great big grin on his face, Keith pulled out a long lighter and lit it up. Kelly dropped the rock in the glass pipe as Keith leaned over, beaming as she took a deep pull on the pipe. Watching the glass pipe fill with smoke, she pulled even harder and deeper. Her eyes began to look upwards and turn glassy. Holding the pipe in her hand, she began to rock back and forth while holding the smoke deep in her lungs. Keith handed Sandra the other pipe, dropped a rock inside for her, and once more lit the lighter. Sandra also took a deep pull while looking at Keith. As her eyes began to close, she pulled harder and harder until the pipe was clear. She exhaled as her eyes went to the top of her head. Kelly stopped long enough to take a long sip of the "Hen," and then she released the smoke from her lungs. When Sandra saw her friend take a drink, she reached down in search of her cup, opened her eyes long enough to pick it up, and took a long swallow.

"That was good," said Kelly, nodding her head. Sandra agreed while sipping on her own drink.

The guys both took hits, but not like the ladies; they wanted to remain in control of the party. Once again, Kelly reached for the still-hot pipe. Keith dropped another rock inside the pipe and lit it up. She pulled even harder this time, as if it was her first time. Sandra followed with another hit for herself. They had been getting high for what seemed like hours, but it had only been twenty minutes. Allen, who was now ready to party, reached over and pulled Sandra down between his legs.

Sandra offered little resistance; she knew it was coming and welcomed it. She quickly unzipped his pants, pulled out his penis and started sucking it with her head bobbing up and down, slowly at first, then faster. She used her tongue and lips in what seemed like a sequential order, soon bringing him to the point of being ready to explode. Keith sat by, watching in awe.

Kelly had seen Sandra's act many time and was not surprised by her performance. But it was now her turn. She relished the idea of being able to outdo her best friend. She didn't wait to be pulled into action; as Keith watched Sandra's performance, she went down on her knees, got between his legs, unzipped his pants, and went to work. Kelly was doing deep-throat maneuvers on him. Both guys looked at each other with their mouths wide open, slobber running from their mouths in disbelief. Sandra and Kelly were laughing inside because they had done this act over a dozen times and always got the same response. The guys were now ready for sex, and they asked for direction to the bedrooms.

Kelly blurted out, "If you want to fuck, it's going to cost you fifty dollars each."

In a calm yet declarative voice, Allen said, "I tell you what. We will give each of you twenty-five dollars and two rocks after we fuck."

"No deal," said Kelly, "You pay us up front, or there will

be no fucking!" The ladies had heard this line before and weren't going for any bull crap. "Pay us now," demanded Kelly.

"Okay, ladies, we will give you twenty-five dollars now and the two rocks later."

"Deal," said Kelly.

Allen gave them both twenty-five dollars apiece, and then he grabbed the light and headed up the staircase. At the top of the stairs, he found the bedrooms and noticed the filthy, nasty-looking mattresses lying on the floor. The pervasive smell of urine and feces ranged throughout the entire second floor. Allen had never seen anything like this in all of his years. He could not believe how nasty the place was. Remembering the blanket and some old newspapers in the trunk of the car, he went down to the car and grabbed them to cover both mattresses. Keith placed the lamp in the middle of the hallway, providing just enough light in each room.

About an hour had gone by when Allen heard a commotion going on between Keith and Kelly. With Sandra in tow, he entered the other bedroom, where they both witnessed Kelly completely naked and smoking from the crack pipe. Keith, who had been drinking heavily, was bleeding from his forehead.

"What happened?" Allen yelled.

"This crazy bitch thought I was asleep and took one hundred dollars out of my pants pocket and is now refusing to give it back to me. She then hit me in the head with that damn pipe!"

As Kelly sat there with the pipe in her mouth, naked as the day she'd come into this world, she said, "Just where am I supposed to be hiding one hundred dollars, up my ass? You've already been there, and we didn't even talk about that being included. He knows there is nothing up there."

Just as she turned her head, pulling as hard as she could on the pipe, not knowing it would be her last hit in life, Keith hit her in the back of her head with his Glock with such tremendous force that her eyes went to the top of her head, and she fell face down onto the floor, dead.

Sandra's eyes opened as big as quarters as she felt that like her friend, this was the end of her life too. She turned to run, but Allen grabbed her by the back of her hair, lifting her small body off the floor and back into the room of death. He choked her until life left her body.

Sandra Nelson and Kelly Starks lost their lives that night. But the only thing the people of Chicago would remember about October 14, 2003, was that the Cubs lost game five and went on to lose game six and a chance to go to the World Series.

~Chapter 3~

Alan and Keith carried the lifeless bodies into the basement, but not before retrieving their twenty-five dollars. They hid the bodies in the coal bin until they could bury them later on that night. Both men knew it would be a problem if the police found the women's bodies full of their DNA, so they traveled to Lowe's Home Improvement Store near 87th and Dan Ryan. Once there, they got into separate lines so as to not draw attention or suspicion to what they were buying. Allen bought two shovels and Keith bought the lime to cover the bodies with. They had heard that if you cover a body under dirt with lime, it would eat up the remains.

Two days later, Sandra Nelson's family called the police and reported her missing. The same officers who'd responded to the disturbance the night the man had refused to leave from their porch, responded to the call once again. The last line of their report read "Known drug user and prostitute." A week later, Kelly Stark's family reported her missing, and a note was added to the bottom of her report with the same information.

For Allen and Keith, life went on. They dumped the Lexus and stole a black BMW. They drove it for about a week and then dumped it for a Buick in hopes it would draw less attention as they searched for their next victim. They often laughed and made jokes about the look on Kelly's face as her body had hit the floor and Sandra's attempt to run as Allen had lifted her skinny ass off the floor, with her legs kicking as if she was running. They thought it was really funny watching the two young ladies die the way they had. The duo would not kill again for at least three months.

When they felt the police had not connected them to the two girls' disappearance, they would often go by "The Den," and if anyone was in the house, they would rob them of their money and drugs, knowing their victims could not call the police. They continued on this path until people stopped coming by the place altogether. Once they had people afraid of going to the house, they kind of cleaned it up a bit. They hid the nice gas lamps inside the house, along with several clean blankets and coverings for the mattresses that they had bought from a second-hand store. They also changed the locks, making it harder for folks to walk in. "The Den" looked almost as if someone lived there.

Around Valentine's Day, Allen met thirty-two-year-old Patricia Lynn Murphy, who was affectionately called Ms. Pat by her close friends. Pat was attending a twelve-step Al-Anon meeting that was designed to help individuals dealing with drug addictions. He befriended her with plans of leading her back into a life of drugs. His strategy was to ask her to have coffee with him after a meeting, which was a common practice for members attending Al-Anon meetings. Coffee was the drink of choice, as opposed to liquor. After attending several meetings, he kind of sat in the back with his head down, hoping not to be noticed or to draw much attention to himself. He finally got up enough nerve to ask her out for coffee, and of course, she agreed. She informed him that two other women were going to join them for coffee also.

As the three ladies entered the coffee shop, one of them got an emergency phone call. She was needed at home right away, which meant the lady who was riding with her had to leave too. Alone, Ms. Pat took a seat and waited for Allen to arrive. When he arrived, he could not believe that she was sitting by herself. They sat and talked for at least an hour when he asked if she needed a ride because it was so late. Ms. Pat did not want to take public transportation this late at night all alone, so she reluctantly accepted the ride rather than wait on the bus.

Once she got into the car, the smell of crack was so strong that she could taste it. The aroma tasted great as she reminisced about her last high. Holding his head down, Allen apologized for his relapsing—knowing all along this was part of his plan.

Pat smiled and said sorrowfully, "I have relapsed several times this year myself."

He then pulled his crack pipe from under the driver's seat and asked if she wanted a hit. He tried to reassure her that everything was going to be okay tomorrow, that they could start fresh all over again together. He also told her he was feeling bad, but if she joined him, he wouldn't feel so bad after all.

"Sure," Pat replied, and she raised the warm pipe to her lips. Within a few minutes, she was sucking the heavy, dark smoke into her lungs. It felt so damn good to get high again. But in the back of her mind, she was feeling disappointed and saddened. She had failed people like her sponsor, who had spent countless hours with her trying to keep her clean, and her doctor, who had warned her that her heart was too weak to continue doing drugs and that it would eventually kill her. It had been two long months since her last time. She asked Allen if he had another rock. He told her he had more at the house, which was only a few minutes away, and he started driving towards "The Den." In the back of his mind, he had gotten what he really wanted, Ms. Pat, and no one had seen him with her.

Allen called Keith to let him know that he was on his way to the house with a lady. Keith responded, telling Allen that he was just about to call him because he had met a homeless white girl name Becky at 95th and Dan Ryan who wanted to get high too, but they needed a ride. Allen told Keith about Pat and that he would be there to pick them up in about fifteen minutes. When they met up, they all introduced themselves, and then they drove to the liquor store and then onto "The Den."

Once inside the house, it was the same old game: start with the drinks, get the girls high, and then take them upstairs for the sex party. However, this time, there was an unexpected change in the plans. Ms. Pat, in the middle of taking a deep pull on her third hit, fell flat on her face onto the floor. There were looks of bewilderment on all their faces as, not knowing what

27

had just happened, Allen turned Pat over. He immediately saw that she was not breathing and that her eyes were closed with no movement. Putting his head and ear on her chest to see if he could hear a heartbeat, he got nothing; she was dead! Her body lay there, lifeless, as the two men tried to decide what to do next. Ms. Pat had suffered a massive heart attack, just as her doctor had predicted.

Keith turned to Allen and said, "That shit there is your problem. Becky and I are on our way upstairs," and he pulled Becky by the arm towards the staircase.

Becky said, "Stop. Is she alright?"

"She's fine." Keith responded. "She just had too much to drink."

Allen took Pat's lifeless body down into the basement and laid her next to the wall near the coal bin. He then headed upstairs, where Keith and Becky were already getting undressed and ready to do the do. Allen walked into the room and began taking off his clothes too.

Becky looked at him and said, "I'm not doing both of you!"

Looking at each other they said, "We share everything,

including you, Ms. Becky!"

Allen jaggedly pushed his penis in her mouth while Keith, who was already inside her, agreed with him.

Becky pushed his penis out of her mouth long enough to ask, "What's going on with the other girl?"

"She passed out. She will be okay by tomorrow morning," Allen replied while pushing his penis back in her mouth.

Keith looked at Allen and said, "You know, this is the first time I ever fucked a white girl."

"This is my first time too," Allen replied.

Becky once again took Allen's penis out of her mouth and asked if they wanted her to call some friends.

"You have some friends who will come to the South Side?" Allen asked.

"Yes, but they are going to want some money and some smack."

"How much are we talking about?" asked Keith.

"Around one hundred dollars apiece," Becky said.

Allen remarked, "We could make a damn movie."

"I have already made a few movies over the last two

years. You can make a lot of money with the right girls, and I know the right girls," she said.

"Can you call them now?" Allen asked.

"It's too late tonight; they are already into what they will be doing, but how about tomorrow?"

Keith replied, "Let me think about it."

An hour later, Becky was passed out cold. The guys talked about making movies for over an hour before they realize how much money the camera equipment would cost. They were now trying to decide on what to do with Becky. They were afraid to kill a white girl for fear of what would happen if they got caught. Keith suggested taking her to a nearby motel and keeping her there for a while. She had no idea where she was, and if she asked about Pat, they would simply say she'd woken up the next morning and gone home.

The next day, they had Becky call several of her friends to ask if they wanted to get high on the South Side of Chicago. They blatantly said no and told her to come back north before something bad happened to her. After two days of trying to get her friends to come south, Allen and Keith gave up and went to "The Den" to get high and have sex with Becky one more time before they killed and buried her next to Ms. Pat in the coal bin.

Patricia Lynn Murphy's family reported her missing several days later, and at the end of her report, it read "Known drug user." Life went on for Allen and Keith as they went out searching for their next victim.

~Chapter 4~

In January of 2004, three full months since Sandra had gone missing, her cousin Walter Best, a former drug dealer from the Roseland community, was contacted by Sandra's parents. They told Walter the whole story, starting with her addiction, then her stealing from them, and now her disappearance and the non-cooperation of the Chicago police department. Walter agreed to come back and see if he could find out what had happened to his cousin. The two of them had grown up together and played as kids, and their mothers were part of a close-knit family who had come to Chicago from the South in hopes of finding a better life. Walter and Sandra had once been close and had often called each other. They called each other "cuz-o."

Walter explained to his aunt and uncle that he had been away from the Chicago streets for three years and a lot had changed since then. His aunt told him he was their last hope of ever finding out what had happened to their little girl. He asked if they had reported her missing to the police, and if so, what the police had been told about the case. Sandra's parents told him that they had heard nothing from the police since reporting Sandra missing.

Walter went to Chicago's Area South Detective Division, located near 111th and Cottage Grove. There he met with Detective Marshall Willis, who had been assigned to her case. The detective informed Walter that he had nothing new to report and that these women, local prostitutes, came and went all the time and sometimes they left the state with hopes of making more money. This was not true in most cases, but it sounded good, and the detective thought it would buy him some time with the families.

Walter considered himself a man of the streets, but he had left the dope game to go to college in search of a better life. He knew what he had to do. He needed to do what the Chicago police were not willing to do. He needed to find his missing cousin Sandra.

Walter started asking questions, like "Where do women go to find men to buy them drugs?" He was told to start with the nightclubs, to talk to the women there and also in the strip clubs. He was told to also talk to women who were looking to get high. He needed to find out who knew Sandra, and maybe who she hung out with, who her friends were, and where they partied.

After three months, Walter had learned a lot about the drug culture and the nightlife and how they came together on the streets of Chicago's South Side. He heard stories from numerous women who'd once lived that life and some who were still living it. These women shared their own personal stories of how they'd gotten started using drugs and some of the things they had lived through. They told him about the men who preyed on women with addictions and how, because some of those women were prostitutes, no one cared if they went missing. They shared stories of friends who were now dead. Some of them knew the men who killed them but were too afraid to tell the police. They told him how they'd had to develop little codes to let one another know if a guy was okay or if he was dangerous or violent. They told him how some guys liked to get high and then would feel bad about their addiction and would beat women up because they were feeling bad.

"We have to know who these guys are in order to survive

out here, Walter," said a woman named Gloria. "I have been out here for ten years trying to stay alive. We have a saying out here: 'That's how the cookie crumbles here in the jungle.' That's how it is out here, a real jungle."

She told Walter that her full name was Gloria Bennett. In turn, he asked her if she could help him find his cousin Sandra. He showed her Sandra's high school graduation picture, stating she had changed a little from being on the streets for more than two years. Gloria looked at the picture and asked if he had a more recent picture, because this photo was more than ten years old and if she had been on the street for two years, she would look very different now. Walter agreed to find a more recent photo if she would meet with him again.

Gloria asked, "Is there anything in it for me?"

"If you help me find my cousin, my family will do what we can."

Gloria and Walter exchanged numbers with the understanding they would stay in contact with each other. Walter called his aunt and told her he needed a more recent picture of Sandra. It took more than a week for his aunt to find one that was up to date. He took the picture to Walgreens and had several copies made so that he could give one to Gloria and anybody else who was willing to help him find Sandra. He contacted her again, and she agreed to meet with him later that night at the bar near 120th and Halsted.

When Walter walked into the bar, Gloria was already there, sitting at the bar and having a drink. She waved Walter over towards her and told him to have a seat. She was wearing a white low-cut blouse that was so tight he wondered how she could breathe in it. She had on a tight, short red leather skirt. Looking down, he noticed her three-inch red high heels with pieces of the patent leather peeling off.

Gloria told Walter that they had to talk fast because she was meeting her date here in twenty minutes. She took one look at the recent picture and said, "I know her. She and this other girl Kelly worked together. You are right; I haven't seen either one of them in a while."

"What do you mean they worked together?" asked Walter.

She looked at him and said, "Remember when I told you that we have a little code out here on the streets? You see, when you work with someone, you look out for each other while out here on these streets."

"Well, do you know Kelly's last name?"

"I don't even know if Kelly's her real name. Like me, some people take on street names. My real name is Mahalia Lee Jackson. Now, imagine that. I changed it to a real nice, easy name to remember, with a little class like they do in Hollywood."

"So you haven't seen this Kelly in a while either?"

"Nope," Gloria responded.

"Has anyone ever come around here looking for either one of them, like the police?"

"Not to my knowledge. No one other than you has ever asked me about either one of these girls. I told you people don't care about you. Once they find out you are a dope fiend and a prostitute too, they don't give a shit about you."

Walter gave her the picture and asked her if she would ask around about both of them. He asked her to see if she could come up with the names of people who knew them or the guys they hung out with.

Gloria looked at Walter and said, "You want me to act like one of those undercover detectives on TV, right? Like a real

Sherlock Holmes? Wow!"

"Just call me if you find out anything. It does not matter the time of day; just call me. You got my number."

Gloria told him he had to leave immediately because she'd spotted her date parking his car. "Hey, before you go, can you leave me a few dollars, if you don't mind?"

"Sure, how about twenty dollars?"

Gloria arched a stern eyebrow in his direction, a look of "What the fuck!" Walter put two twenty dollars bills in Gloria's hand, which brought a huge smile to her face.

"Be safe," said Walter as Gloria walked away in her tight red skirt. He hadn't noticed before, but as she walked away, he saw how shapely she was, with a big, round ass!

The next morning, Walter Best walked into the police station and asked the uniformed female officer who was working the desk, with a nametag that read "Wallace," if he could speak with Detective Willis.

Officer Wallace picked up the phone and called upstairs, where Detective Willis actually worked. After a few minutes went by, she hung up the phone, turned, and informed Walter that Detective Willis would not be in today, that it was his day off.

"Is there anyone else that I might be able to talk to about this case?"

Officer Wallace had a look of unconcern on her face as she called upstairs to ask if there were anyone who could come down and talk to this man who was getting on her last nerve. She hung up the phone and asked Walter to have a seat, stating that someone would be down to talk to him in a few minutes.

Fifteen minutes later, a white man dressed in an suit walked over to her desk and asked, "Who wants to talk to Detective Willis?"

Officer Wallace pointed to Walter, who had already gotten up out of his seat. The man introduced himself as Sergeant Ray Flynn, supervising sergeant for missing persons. Walter asked if there was a place they could talk, and the sergeant suggested his office. Once there, Walter went on to explain why he wanted to speak with Detective Willis. Sergeant Flynn took notes and informed him that Detective Willis would be back to work in two days and that he would call Walter upon his return. Walter left the police station feeling he hadn't accomplished a thing; it was just like Gloria had said about dope fiends and whores.

Three days later, Detective Willis called Walter and apologized for not getting back to him sooner, explaining that he had been unusually busy the last couple of days. The sergeant listened as Walter went into detail as to what he had learned over the last three months.

"Do you have any names?" asked the detective.

"Just one, sir, and her name is supposedly Kelly."

"No last name?"

"Actually, I believe she's missing too," Walter replied. "She's a black female, and I think she's around the same age as my cousin Sandra."

Detective Willis thanked Walter for his help and said he would get back with him when he had something solid. Once again, Walter felt he had been blown off by the police

~Chapter 5~

It would be two weeks before Walter heard from Gloria again. At two in the morning, his cell phone rang, and it was her. She apologized for calling so late and said she might have something for him.

Still half-sleep, he asked her, "What do you have?"

"First, I need to know if you have any money!"

Walter acted as if he had not heard her ask him for money at two in the damn morning. She began to whisper into the phone that she really had something and she needed fifty dollars to get high because she was feeling really bad.

"I don't have fifty dollars at two o'clock in the morning, and if I did, how would I give it to you?"

"Please, man, I need the fifty dollars now! I will suck your dick for it if you want me to. I just need the money!"

"What do you have that's so important that you would call me this time of morning for fifty damn dollars!"

"I have a guy who told me he saw Sandra and Kelly with these two crazy motherfuckers."

"What two crazy motherfuckers? You got a name or names?"

"If you just meet us at the gas station on 115th Halsted in fifteen minutes, you can ask him yourself. But he's not going to be around here for long. The both of us are trying to get high, and if somebody pulls up and wants to do some business, we're gone."

Walter slipped into his sweatsuit and, with the fifty dollars in his pocket, was off to meet Gloria and her friend. As Walter pulled into the gas station, he recognized Gloria's tight red leather skirt and, what was most obvious, her big ass as she leaned inside the passenger side window of a car parked at the gas station. He blew the horn, causing her to look up. Once she recognized it was Walter, she walked away from the car, which took off. As she walked in his direction, he could see her eyes were glassy, and she was stumbling as she neared his car. He could tell she was high. She walked to the passenger side of his car and began pulling on the door handle.

Once inside the car, she asked him, "You got my money?"

Walter, trying his best not to get upset or angry, asked,

"Where is the guy?"

Gloria pointed to a skinny, malnourished-looking young man standing in the middle of the street, obstructing what little traffic there was at two thirty in the morning. She leaned out of the window and yelled, "Hey, Snowball, our ride is here! Come and get in the car!"

Walter turned to Gloria and asked, "What you mean our ride is here? You never once mentioned I was supposed to take you somewhere, let alone put some guy in my car."

Walter looked up and saw Snowball walking toward his car. He looked a damn mess! His shirt was hanging outside of his pants, which were hanging down because he lacked a belt to hold them up. He looked like he hadn't taken a bath in months. Snowball was now pulling on the car door's latch while mumbling under his breath. Walter could see he was missing all of his teeth, and to top it off, he was foaming at the mouth.

Gloria turned to Walter and said, "Let him in. He's okay."

Walter sat for a minute, trying to decide what to do next. Before he could make his mind up, Gloria had turned around and unlocked the rear door for Snowball. As the door opened, the smell confirmed what Walter was thinking: Snowball needed a serious bath, like yesterday.

As Snowball made his way into the back seat, he asked Gloria, "Is this the connection?"

She looked back at him like he had said something really wrong. "No," she replied. "He's the guy looking for the two crazy motherfuckers you told me about."

Snowball thought about what she said for a moment and then told Walter, "I don't want to mess around with them. They are certified crazy."

With that, Snowball started to get out the car. Gloria looked back at him and said, "Get your ass back in this damn car. We are not looking for them now. He just wants to know who they are and where he can find them."

Walter still could not muster up the strength to tell Snowball to get back in the car. However, Gloria convinced Snowball to get back in while Walter was busy letting down all the windows. Finally, with Snowball in tow, Gloria told Walter to drive.

"Where we are going?" Walter asked.

"We're going to 113th and Normal. That's were my connection is. We can talk as you're driving. Let's go."

While driving east on 115th Street, Walter asked Snowball to tell him something about the guys, but Snowball would only repeat, "They are some crazy motherfuckers."

Walter pulled over to the curb. He turned to looked at Gloria and Snowball and said, "Before I give either one of you a dime, you're going to tell me more than that they are two crazy motherfuckers. I got that part. What the hell are their names?"

"One of them is called or goes by the name Crazy A," said Snowball reluctantly. "All the dope boys and whores around here know them by Crazy A and his boy."

"I need names, addresses, descriptions of what they look like and what kind of car they are driving, and anything else," said Walter.

Snowball looked him in the eye and said, "Just ask any of these dope boys. They can tell you exactly who they are, and they're always driving a different car every time you see them."

Walter started driving again; turning left onto Normal, and about a halfway down the block, Gloria said, "Stop! You give me the money now," and she held her hand out.

Snowball opened the rear door as she sat there with her

hand out, waiting for the money. Once Walter placed the money in her hand, they both disappeared into the night. Walter did not know if he had just gotten played or if Gloria and Snowball had been telling the truth. At this point, he was out of fifty dollars either way.

~Chapter 6~

The next day, Walter called some people he knew and asked if he could have a word with them. He also arranged to meet with an old friend who was big in the drug scene, near Roseland and the West Pullman area. The time was set for five o'clock at the car wash on 115th and Halsted. Walter got there a little early, and he sat in his car, thinking things over. At five o'clock precisely, a big white BMW pulled up next to him. It was his boy Shun.

Shun got out of his car and said to Walter, "What's going on, dog!"

"You, player, you're what's going on," answered Walter.

He and Shun were both out of their cars when Shun said, "long time, nigger. What you need?"

Walter told Shun about his cousin Sandra and how he was looking for these two guys named Crazy A and his boy.

Like everyone else, all Shun could say was, "Those two are some crazy motherfuckers!"

"So I heard," said Walter. "Do you know their names?"

"One name is Allen, and the other Keith. But let me tell you something. You don't want to fuck with them two niggers. They are dangerous! They have probably killed ten niggers and a dozen whores. Those two ain't no joke! If you fuck with them, you better be ready to die." Looking Walter in the eyes, he said, "When you called me, I thought you were ready to get back in the game, but now that I know what you want, let me give you some free advice—and usually free advice is not worth listening to, but hear me and hear me good—let it go! Those two niggers are truly fucked up, and they will kill your black ass if they thought you were looking for them or sending the police their way." Shun walked back to his car, shaking his head and repeatedly saying, "Man, let it go, let it go!"

Walter sat in his car, right there at 115th and Halsted, for an hour thinking, *what have I gotten myself into?* He remembered Snowball saying that he didn't want any part of the two guys, and now Shun, a big time player, wanted no part either. *What the fuck have I gotten myself into?* was all he could think.

Around seven o'clock, he called Shun back and asked for another meeting.

"Where are you?" Shun asked.

"I'm in the same spot you left me at."

"Stay there. I'll be right back."

When Shun arrived, Walter was sitting with his head down. Shun went over to him and asked, "Are you alright, man?"

Walter shook his head. "I don't know what to do right now."

Shun suggested taking a ride in his car, because he needed to be careful. Walter parked his car and got in the car with his friend. Shun headed south on Halsted as they talked. They started off talking about the good old days when they'd both been young and hustling dope. Shun told Walter how proud of him he was for getting out of the game and going back to school. He shared how things were different now than they'd been back then and how there was no respect for the game today. It was now every man for himself, and that was why those two crazy motherfuckers were able to keep doing what they did, because no one was holding them accountable. Everyone just kept turning their heads as Allen and Keith killed person after person. Shun told Walter he was going to talk to some people, and he warned Walter to never mention to anyone what they had talked about, because they both could end up dead.

Three days later, they met for breakfast at the Pancake House on Western. Shun asked Walter how he knew Sandra was dead.

"I don't know for sure, but the family has not heard from her in three months. It's not like her to not check in, despite her addiction, which means she is probably dead."

Shun looked at Walter and said, "Okay, let's say she's dead. Where is the body, then? Because, with no body, you have no crime. I don't mean any harm Walt, but she's just another missing bitch, if you know what I mean."

"Shun, you said they have killed at least ten people, right? So tell me, were the bodies ever found?"

"Yes, because they wanted them to be found to send a message that they were not to be fucked with."

"What about all the women they killed? What happened to their bodies?"

"Bro, they just disappeared one day, and nobody heard from them again, just like Sandra."

"So we need to follow them and see where they go, or better yet, let's give them a whore and follow her and see where they go."

"Man, you talking about some TV shit! What whore do you know that's stupid enough to do some shit like that?"

"Then let's ask the police if they have undercover people, right?"

"Man, you trippin'! I can't afford to have the police around me; I got business to take care of."

The following day, Gloria called Walter. She needed one hundred dollars right away. Her tricks had been extremely slow, and she needed to get high. She wanted to sell some good information about the killers, but he had to give her one hundred dollars for it. Walter looked at his phone and wondered, *Has this bitch lost her mind? Why would I pay her one hundred dollars for anything!*

"Listen, man," said Gloria, "I found out where those two crazy motherfuckers take their whores to get high and fuck them."

Walter jumped up and asked her if she knew where the location was.

Gloria paused for a moment and said, "Snowball does. His crazy ass followed them to the house. I told him he was stupid and that they would kill him if they knew what he was doing."

"Why do you like Snowball so much?"

"He's my younger brother," she said sadly. "He was trying to help me get straight and got caught up. We've been watching each other's back for the past five years, but I'm tired, and he is sick with the HIV virus and can't afford the medicine. Eventually, my brother's going to die."

"Where is he at now? I need the address of where those guys go to get high."

"I asked him to meet up with us at 115th and Halsted, where he likes to hang out. People know Snowball around there, and Crazy A and his boy are less likely to do any harm to him. We have got to find him before they kill him!"

Walter had been warned by everyone who knew these guys that they were not to be taken lightly. He was ignoring all the good advice he'd been given. He was ignoring the feeling inside his gut, which was screaming, *Don't get involved!*

Gloria began to cry profusely, as he could feel her pain

coming through the phone. He told her he was on his way as he wiped the drop that fell from his eye.

They looked for Snowball for hours. They talked to anyone who was still on the streets at that hour. They spoke to homeless folks, street whores, dope fiends, just about anybody who was out there, but with no luck; Snowball had not been seen or heard from. Gloria feared the worst that somehow the duo had found out what he'd been doing and had killed him.

Chapter 7

Two days later, the body of Reggie L. Jackson, aka Snowball, was found stuffed in a garbage can in the alley behind the car wash near 115th and Halsted. His throat had been cut from ear to ear. Walter wondered if he had talked and if he had told the people who killed him what, why, and who he'd been doing it for. Snowball had no life insurance, so there was no funeral or memorial service held for him. Gloria promised to get the bastards back at any cost, even if it meant losing her own life. Walter told her they needed a plan, one that would lead them to where Allen and Keith got high and played.

Later on, at two o'clock in the morning, Walter's phone rang. It was Gloria. She started off by apologizing for calling so late, but went straight to the point. Checking her phone messages, she realized that she had missed a call from Snowball just before he was killed. He had left the address of where Allen and Keith went to get high. The address was 10972 South Eggleston. It was an abandoned, boarded-up house.

Walter picked Gloria up, and they drove to the house to

take a look. Driving by, they both got an eerie feeling. Walter parked down the street and walked to the house, with Gloria following him. When they got to the house, they looked around, but they were too afraid to go inside. They checked the doors and noticed they were all locked. The house looked as if it had been boarded up for years.

"Do you want to break in and look around?" asked Gloria.

"Hell no! Not by myself."

"Well then, should we call the police?"

"Walter gave her a sharp look and said, "What should I tell them, that this is where the two crazy motherfuckers come to get high and have sex with street whores and kill them? Gloria, you're just as crazy as them!"

The next morning, he headed back to the police station to ask for Detective Willis and was greeted at the front desk by Officer Wallace. Taking one look at him she said, "Didn't they tell you they would call you if they had something new?"

Walter frowned at her and said, "I have something very important to tell him about the case, and I need to talk with him now!"

Stunned, she called upstairs and asked Detective Willis to come down and talk with this man before she had to give him the business. A few minutes later, Detective Willis came down the stairs with his coat and hat in his hand. He looked over at Walter and said, "Make it quick. I have another job to do."

Walter walked alongside the detective as he made his way towards the parking lot. He explained that he thought he had found the house that the two men used to get high and have sex. He also shared that it might be the place where the bodies had been buried.

The detective turned to him and asked, "What the fuck are you talking about? What two men? What house? And what is this shit you talking about, dead bodies?"

Walter tried to explain, but the detective was not hearing him. "Listen, before we can go into someone's house, we need a search warrant. Do you know what that is, Mr. Best?" Having made his point, Detective Willis got in his car and drove off without saying another word, and Walter left the Chicago police station feeling like he'd been blown off again.

When Shun heard the news about Snowball, he called Walter and asked if he had heard yet.

"I already know," said Walter.

"I told you those motherfuckers were dangerous and would kill a nigger in a heartbeat."

"Yes, you told me man, but that still doesn't make it right what these niggers are doing." Walter then expressed his fear that Snowball had told them what he was doing and who he was doing it for. "I'm afraid that they might be coming for me next, and I don't know what to do." He explained how the police were not trying to help him find Sandra's killers.

Shun asked, "Do you remember Henry Long from high school? The quarterback of our team?"

"Yeah, what about him?"

"Well, he works in the gang unit over there on 111th Street."

"How do you know this?" Walter asked.

"I make my living on these streets, man. You got to know who is what, and that includes the police too."

"Do you think he might help me?"

"I don't know, man; all you can do is ask at this point."

"I remember him well. We all graduated from high school together. In fact, he and I had several classes together."

The next morning, Walter walked into the same police station and was met by the same officer, who upon recognizing him, begin to shake her head. He wondered if she ever took a damn day off.

She said sarcastically, "Let me guess, you want to see Detective Willis, right?"

"No ma'am," replied Walter. "I would like to see a gang officer named Henry Long."

She gave Walter a long look and then said, "He works nights, and he won't be in until five pm. But I tell you what, Mr. Best, let me check to see if he is working tonight because I would hate to see you keep coming back for no reason."

Picking up the phone, she called upstairs to confirm that Officer Long was scheduled to work that night. When she got the answer that yes, he would be, Walter thanked her very politely, turned and walked out of the station feeling completely exhausted with Chicago's police department.

Returning around fifteen minutes before five, Walter watched as Officer Wallace prepared to leave for the day. Before leaving, she told the relief officer that Walter was looking for gang specialist Henry Long and that the officer would be in shortly.

"He can have a seat and wait," she told the relief officer.

Walter thanked her as he took a seat. Upon walking out the door, she rolled her eyes at him. After waiting for over an hour, Walter politely asked the desk officer if Mr. Long was in. The desk officer finally called upstairs, and a few minutes later, Henry Long came down the stairs.

Henry took one look at Walter and said, "Walter Best, my man!" Walter was surprised that Henry remembered him. Henry asked him how he was doing and said that he'd heard Walter was leaving town to go back to school. "News travels fast around here, and bad news travels even faster. How can I help you, Walt?"

Walter asked, "Is there someplace we can go and talk?"

Henry gave him a long look and said, "It's that serious?"

"Yes," replied Walter.

"Okay, follow me to my office."

Once inside, they began to talk. Walter told Henry everything he knew about Sandra, Allen, Keith, and Snowball. Henry sat there, amazed at what Walter had learned in three months off the streets. Henry asked Walter for his number and told him that he would get back with him after he'd done some work on what he had just learned.

Walter left the station for the first time feeling that he was going to get some help from Chicago's finest. As he drove west on 111th, he stopped at the light on King Drive, and a car pulled up next to him with two guys looking straight at him. As the light changed, Walter drove on, but he kept a close eye on the car next to him. It was an older white BMW. As Walter sped up, so did the car next to him. *Are they following me? Is that Allen and Keith in the car?* All those questions raced through his mind as he drove faster down 111th. He made a quick left turn on Michigan and then a quick right on 112th. Looking in the rear view mirror, he could see the car still following him. He then decided to go back to the police station, feeling that was his only hope of living to see another day. As he looked in the rear view mirror, the car had gotten so close that if he stopped, they would run right into the back of him.

Approaching King Drive, the light was red. *Should I stop, or should I go through the light?* As he slowed down for the light, the car pulled up next to him with the driver's window down. He saw the passenger reach over the driver and point his gun, firing in Walter's direction.

Walter stepped on the gas; he knew he had to get back to the police station, and now. Flying right through the light at Cottage Grove and Ellis Street, he turned on two wheels into the police parking lot. He noticed the BMW drive on, heading straight and then turning onto the expressway headed south. As he got out of his car, he could see his car had three bullets holes in the passenger side door.

Running into the station, he explained to the desk sergeant what had just happened and demanded to speak with Officer Long. Henry ran down the stairs and asked, "Walter, what happened?" Swiftly taking Walter up to his office, he told him to catch his breath and have a seat.

Walter looked at Henry and said, "I thought I was going to die! Those motherfuckers really are crazy! They followed me back to the fucking police station! Who does shit like that!" Henry told him to calm down. "Calm down! DO you understand what I'm saying! They just tried to kill me right in front of a police station!"

"I will be right back," Henry said. When he returned, he had two other officers with him. Henry started off by telling

Walter that between the three of them, they had over twenty years of gang experience on the south side of Chicago and they had never heard of Allen or Keith. He then went on to say that they, as a unit, found it hard to believe that two killers could be out there that long without the unit knowing about them. He also said he'd had their names run through the police department's computer system and had found no matches or any evidence that the two even existed.

Walter looked at all three officers and said, "Go take a look at my car and see for yourself if they exist."

All four men walked down to the parking lot and examined the car and the three fresh bullet holes on the passenger side. Walter looked at Henry and asked, "What do I have to do to get some help around here, get killed?"

Henry and his fellow officers now believed him. They all went back inside the station. Henry asked his sergeant, Charles Joyner to meet with them. After the meeting with the sergeant, he called in his entire team, which was comprised of ten men and two women. A total of twelve officers were now on the case. Sergeant Joyner would lead the mission. The very first thing they had to do was hit the house on Eggleston that Walter had told them about.

It was like watching the police on TV now. Sergeant Joyner stood in front of the room, at the blackboard, with a picture of a house. The sergeant assigned every man and woman to a position around the house. He even brought in some uniformed officers to protect the perimeter while he and his troops took the house. Walter felt that after three months, he was finally getting real police service.

The time was ten pm as Walter waited inside the car right outside the perimeter. He watched as the gang unit did their thing. One by one, they circled the house and then went in. Within ten minutes, it was over. They had searched the whole house and found no one inside.

Sergeant Joyner walked over to Walter and told him, "No one was in the house, but it has a smell of death." He called for the cadaver dogs to come and smell if there were any dead bodies in the house. In a few minutes, the dogs arrived and had a hit. The house was now a homicide scene. The police began yellow taping the area around the house.

Sergeant Joyner walked over to Walter and told him they were done. Walter asked, "What do you mean, we are done?"

The sergeant told him it was now in the hands of the homicide detective and that he needed Walter to sit tight until the detective came over to fill him in on what was happening

~Chapter 8~

Area South's homicide/sex unit was one of the most elite inside of the detective division. Most detectives in the unit had at least ten years on the job as officers and two more years of experience as a detective. You had to almost audition in order to be accepted into this specialized unit that required one's ability to pay close attention to minor details at crime scenes. Your ability to write reports had to be first rate and impeccable. The reports would be read by, assistant state attorneys, judges, and defense attorneys who were looking for any inconsistency they could use in defense of their clients.

For years, the unit was mostly staffed with white detective before finally being integrated in the late 1980s, and for that reason, the unit had its problems. More of their cases had been overturned by the Supreme Court, than any other department in the country, which was the reason for the change. When it was announced that the unit was going to be integrated, black, brown, and female detectives started applying. Most applicants were rejected because of their lack of writing skills.

Second-generation police officers whose fathers were detectives had a clear advantage. The Wright family was one of those families whose fathers had taken home reports written by some of the best detectives in the unit at the time. They studied these reports for both style and substance. This was a case of imitation, which was the greatest form of flattery. Richard Wright Jr. was the first black detective, followed by Eugene Patterson, who was also a second-generation police detective. Others would eventually follow their lead into the unit.

It was around ten thirty before the first detectives arrived at the crime scene. Detective Richard Wright and his partner Detective Felicia Duplassis arrived, and then came Detective Eugene Patterson and his partner Kenneth Byrd. They called themselves "The Murder Police." They asked one of the marked police vehicles to take Walter back to the area and not to let him go. Walter was put in a little room, where he sat for hours. He asked if he could leave and come back. The uniformed officer said, "I'm sorry, but the dicks said no." Walter then asked if he was under arrest. The officer repeated no again and reminded Walter that he couldn't leave either.

"Well, if this is the case, can I at least make a phone

call?"

"Not now, but maybe later when the dicks get here."

"What are they doing?" Walter asked.

"They are processing the crime scene, and that could take a while."

"Can I get some food and something to drink around here? I'm starving."

About an hour later, a uniformed policeman handed Walter a bag from McDonald's that had a Big Mac and french fries in it, along with a soda. A full eight hours later, at eight thirty am, Detective Wright and Detective Duplassis walked into the holding room where Walter had been sitting all night. They introduced themselves and asked him to tell them his story. For the first time, Walter felt like they were trying to blame him for what they had found inside that house.

"Do I need a lawyer?" he asked.

"You tell us Walter; do you think you need one?"

Walter was now questioning himself as to how he'd gotten himself involved in the first place. Then, with a smile on her face, Detective Duplassis said, "No, man, we were just fucking with you. We talked to your friend, Gang Specialist

Henry Long, and he filled us in on what was going on."

Walter thought Detective Duplassis looked sort of young to be a detective. She looked to be around twenty-five years old and stood around five foot nine, tall for a woman. She was very light skinned, almost white looking. Her hair was cut short, but you could see it was beautiful under a black tan she wore sideways like the French. She sported a long black Christian Dior trench coat. Once she took off her coat, it revealed how stylish she dressed, and Walter took notice. She was wearing a black pinstripe pantsuit with a white blouse that had a long collar that landed over her shoulders. Tucked into the jacket pocket was a neat white square. A pair of black loafers by Vince Cameo complimented her outfit.

She spoke with a light accent because she'd been born and raised in New Orleans, Louisiana. She actually looked like she could be Creole. Her fellow officers called her Frenchie because she'd grown up in the French Quarter. She had this walk that reminded you of an athlete walking back to the bench during a timeout in the middle of a game. Frenchie had played basketball in high school and while attending college on a scholarship at the University of Tulane. She'd been a point guard who could shoot with the best of them. In her senior year, she'd taken her team to the sweet sixteen before they'd been beaten by Baylor, who was National Champions that year. She had come to Chicago ten years ago for the first time to visit her cousin Joyce, who at the time had been studying for the Chicago police exam. Joyce had convinced Frenchie to take the exam and two years later, both of them had been in the police academy together. Within five years on the job as an officer, she'd made detective. Her first two years as a detective, she'd worked property crimes, and two years later, she'd been asked to work homicide with "The Murder Police" team.

Her partner, Richard Wright Jr., was a veteran of twenty years, and in most cases, the lead detective. He was a second-generation policeman, whose father and uncle had both been Chicago police detectives. His twin brother Robert, was also on the job, working in the detective division too. One of their cousins also worked in Area South, while the fourth member of their family was waiting for the next class to begin. In fact, if you called the Area and asked for Detective Wright, you would be asked which one. Richard went by the nickname Richie.

Walter wanted to know if they'd found his cousin

Sandra's body. Frenchie explained they had found four bodies in the basement but had not identified any of them or their cause of death. She wanted to know everything he knew about Allen and Keith. Walter described them like everyone else he had talked to had: "They are two crazy motherfuckers!"

"We know that, sir. We need their first and last names. Do you have an address? What kind of car were they driving when they shot at you? Was there a plate on the car?"

Walter looked at the detective's sideways and said, "Do you really think I was trying to get their license plate while they were shooting at me?"

Richie was trying to keep calm; he asked, "Could you give our artist a description of them? Maybe you can help us with a composite drawing of what they looked like."

Walter shook his head in disgust. Finally, he said, "I am not trying to be funny, but all I saw was two crazies from the waist up shooting in my direction. The driver was brown skinned and the passenger was a little darker, with a crazy look in his eyes. He was mean mugging me."

Frenchie asked him, "How did they know you were at the police station?"

"I don't know!" Walter shouted.

"Did you tell anyone you were going to the police?"

Walter though about it for a minute and said, "I told Gloria."

"Who the hell is Gloria," asked Frenchie.

"She's the prostitute I met while looking for Sandra. Gloria and her now dead brother led me to these guys."

Both detectives looked at each other, and Frenchie asked, "How did the brother die?"

"He was found in a garbage can behind the car wash near 115th and Halsted two days ago."

The detectives made eye contact, indicating it was time to stop the interview until they had a few more facts. After making a couple of phone calls, they returned a short time later holding a file with a picture of Snowball stuffed head first in a garbage can. They had been off work the last two days so that meant Eugene and Kenneth must have caught the case.

Frenchie looked at Walter and asked, "Why would she tell them you were going to the police if she is your friend?"

"They must have caught her and made her talk."

"Do you have her number?"

"Yes, I do," said Walter.

"Then call her and ask her."

Walter just stared at the detective's and said, "Your guys took my phone."

A few minutes later, Frenchie returned with his phone saying, "Sorry about that, we have procedures we have to follow."

Walter took his phone, searched Gloria's number, and called her. The phone rang and rang until the voice message picked up saying, "This is Gloria, and I have been waiting on your call. I'm available. Just leave a number or call me back. Bye!" They all looked at each other, and like the detectives, Walter was thinking, *Could they have killed her too?*

Frenchie took a different approach to the situation. "She probably has a date right now and can't answer the phone. You know it's not polite to talk with your mouth full."

"Real funny," said Walter. "Can we go out and look for her?"

Richie and Frenchie asked him where would they look for his prostitute friend at this hour. Walter said, "Every time she asked me to meet her, she was near or at 115th and Halsted.

Let's go there!"

Frenchie reminded him that it was nine am in the morning and that they call them women of the night for a reason: they come out at night. Walter asked if he could go home and take a shower and change his clothes. They agreed, but they were not letting their only lead get killed, so they were coming too.

The two detectives took Walter home. While waiting on him to change clothing, Frenchie called detectives Patterson and Byrd and asked them to come by Walter's house for a meeting.

When the other two detectives arrived, Richie went out and spoke with them. He'd known them for years and had a lot of respect for them. Detective Patterson, who also came from a police family, always felt at ease with his childhood friend Richie Wright. They were the sons of real policemen, which was what they called themselves. Eugene and Kenneth had been working together for over five years. They'd first met in high school over ten years ago. They had played Chicago high school basketball against each other six times during their four years in school. They'd faced each other twice for the city championship. They were the real police. They had a reputation for solving tough murder cases.

The two detectives talked to Richie, who brought them up to speed about their witness and what he knew. They talked about the case of the homeless guy, Reggie Jackson, aka Snowball, who'd been found in the garbage can, and how his death might be related. Eugene explained how they'd found the body and what he believed was the cause of death. Reggie Jackson's throat had been cut from ear to ear. His hands had been tied behind his back with black duct tape, and then he'd been thrown into a garbage can.

As the detectives were going over the case, they received a call that a body of what appeared to be a female prostitute had just been found in a garbage can in the alley of 120th and Normal, face down with her naked ass exposed. They all turned and looked at Walter, who had just showered, changed clothes, and was walking towards their car.

Eugene reminded them that they had not finished processing the house with the four dead women yet. With a look of total disbelief, Kenneth asked, "Are you telling me these two cases might be related?"

From inside the doorway of Walter's house, Frenchie called, "What the fuck is going on out there!" Richie looked at her and asked if she would step into his office for a minute. A few minutes later, Frenchie had all the information she needed.

"What should we do with Walter here?" asked Eugene.

Frenchie said, "He's going with us. I'm thinking it's his girlfriend Gloria."

Eugene turned to look at Walter and said, "His girlfriend?"

"No, it's just a joke between us," said Frenchie.

All four detectives left, along with Walter, heading to the alley behind 120th, near Normal.

~Chapter 9~

Upon their arrival, several blue and white cars blocking the alley on both ends, met them. People lined up on both sides of the alley, trying to get a look at what was going on in back of their houses. The yellow tape circled off the crime scene. The detectives got out of their car and started walking towards the garbage cans telling Walter to come with them.

"Why do I need to go? I don't want all these people seeing me talking to the police."

Frenchie gave Walter that certain look and said, "We need you to come with us."

Still not understanding why he needed to go with them, Walter got close enough to see a body hanging out of a garbage can. He recognized her ass even before he saw the short red skirt and red high heels. Walter lost control and screamed out, "That's Gloria! I know that outfit anywhere. She was wearing it a few days ago." What he really wanted to say was that he knew that ass anywhere, but he did not think they would understand.

Frenchie, along with the other detectives, looked at

Walter and wondered how he was able to identify her without seeing her face. Then it hit her; it must be her ass. Walter turned and headed back to the car, where he took a seat in the back with his head bowed and started to cry. Eugene told Richie and Frenchie that this was exactly how they'd found Snowball's body, and that the cases were now all connected.

Richie went to Walter and said, "It's time for you to go home, and we will get back with you later. Right now we have to process this crime scene."

Walter looked at all four detectives and said, "Hell to the no! Those two crazy motherfuckers are still out there, and they might know where I live. I ain't going nowhere. You guys have to put me into some kind of witness protection housing or something."

Frenchie asked him, "What if we assigned a marked police car to your house?"

"Hell no! That's telling everybody on my block that I'm working with the police. I have to live there after this shit is over, if I'm alive."

"Okay, we will get you a hotel room."

"Not here in this city. No ma'am, unless its downtown

with a police guard standing outside my room."

Richie explained to Walter that they did not have the authority to give him what he was asking for, but would do everything in their power to get an approval for him. By late afternoon, the higher ups had authorized a room downtown and a guard outside the door twenty-four seven, or until Allen and Keith were arrested. Richie had a marked car take Walter back to the station while they processed the new crime scene. He also called his sergeant, told him what they needed for Walter, and asked for his help.

Later that night, Walter was escorted home, by several plainclothes officers, in unmarked cars. He was given enough time to pack up some clothes and any personal items he would need for the next few days, or until they arrested Allen and Keith. Walter arrived at the Hyatt Hotel downtown at around eight pm, and he was given a key to room 911.

"Is this some kind of omen or just plain bad luck?" he asked. "Either way, I want a different room."

This time, he was given 1115. *Another omen*, he thought, as he looked at the clerk who immediately asked, "How about 825?"

"Great, I'll take it."

Once inside his room, Walter checked outside his door, and yes, there was a plainclothes police officer standing watch. He could breathe again knowing he could get a good night's sleep. That lasted about two hours, when he received a call from Richie, who asked how was he doing and if his room was okay. Richie asked Walter to call them when he felt like talking.

Walter said, "Can we do this in the morning, around nine am?"

"Sure, but we'll be coming back to the police station because of the magnitude of this case."

"Why, what's going on?"

"We will talk in the morning," replied Richie. "Get a good night's sleep."

Walter was up around seven am, ready and waiting to get started. He had no idea what lay ahead. The first surprise happened as he approached the unmarked police car and was asked to sit in the front seat. Then he noticed a second unmarked car following them. Noticing the unusual amount of security he was being given, Walter wondered if something had happened.

As the cars approached the station, he could not have imagined in a thousand years what he was seeing. Every TV and radio station in the metropolitan Chicago area had a van and two or three reporters camped out in front of the police station. It looked like there were over a hundred reporters trying to get their questions answered by the police about these murders.

One of the detectives turned to Walter and said, "I have an overcoat and a hat for you to put on. We want you to look like a police officer as we get out of the car. We are going to park in the rear lot, behind the station. We don't want people to know who you are just yet, if you don't mind."

Walter was okay with this idea, and deep down inside, he was hoping they could pull this off. He put the coat on, pulling it up around his neck. He then placed the hat on his head, pulling it down, but not too far. A few minutes later, they were walking into the police station, passing by the reporters without anyone discovering who he was.

As he passed by the front desk, he said, "Good morning, Officer Wallace."

She turned and recognized Walter, but she just smiled,

shook her head, and continued with her work. Once in their office, the detectives began trying to put a plan together on how they were going to apprehend these deadly killers.

Richie turned to Walter and asked, "How did you find them?"

Walter replied, "They found me."

"Let's start from the beginning," Richie continued. "Who did you talk to that led you to find out their names?"

Walter quickly replied, "Gloria and Snowball, who are both dead."

"Was their anyone else who helped you?"

Walter thought about Shun, but because his friend sold drugs, he could not give them his name without talking with Shun first. Walter explained his dilemma and asked for a little time to work it out. Richie explained they did not have any more time; they needed to act now and get these guys off the street before they killed someone else. With this kind of pressure, what could Walter do? He asked if he could call his friend Shun and see if he would meet with them, or at least hear what he had to say about meeting with the police.

Walter call Shun's cell phone, but there was no answer.

After several attempts, they realized he was not answering Walter's calls. Frenchie asked Walter if he knew where Shun lived.

"No," Walter replied, "but I think his mother lives in same house he grew up in, a ranch house on 104th and Wallace."

"Let's go," said Frenchie.

As they all headed down the stairs, Walter stopped and told the detectives he did not think it was a good ideal for him and four detectives to go running up to her door, and they agreed. The plan was to drive past the house and Walter would point it out. They would then park their car around the corner, and he and Frenchie, together, would walk up to the door and ring the bell. Eugene and Kenneth would be parked in the alley behind the house just in case. Frenchie would keep her radio open so they could hear the conversation.

"Walter," said Frenchie, "you will do the talking with Shun's mother. You just need to get in touch with Shun; that's all we want. He is not in any kind of trouble, but we need to talk with him right away."

~Chapter 10~

Walter, with Frenchie at his side, rang the doorbell. A few minutes later, to everyone's surprise, Shun answered the door. "What the hell are you doing here, and who is this bitch you brought to my mama's house!"

Frenchie pushed her way into the house, followed by Walter. Shun looked at her and asked, "Bitch, you the police!"

"Yes, I am, and I need you to calm down, sir."

Shun's mother came from the back of the house and asked, "What going on?"

Frenchie asked Shun if he had any weapons on him. He told her he didn't, but she searched him anyway, patting him down. Satisfied he was telling the truth, she raised her radio to her mouth and said, "I'm in." She then asked Shun's mother, "Is there anyone else in the house?" His mother shook her head, and Frenchie asked her to open the back door. When she did, Detective Patterson and Byrd walked in and began searching the house to see if anyone was there. Within minutes, they gave an all clear, and Richie walked in through the front door. He asked Frenchie if she had searched Shun. She replied yes, but Richie told her to do it again.

Shun looked at Walter and blurted out, "You got that dope fiend and whore killed, and now you trying to get me and my mama killed! I told your ass not to fuck with them two niggers! I told you they were some crazy motherfuckers!"

Simultaneously, Richie and Frenchie told Shun to calm down, that everything was cool because no one had seen them come in. Frenchie told the mother that if she wanted to wait in her bedroom, she could, but couldn't use the phone while they were there. The mother nervously went to her room and shut her bedroom door.

Richie turned towards Shun, looked him in the eye, and told him, "Listen to me. We don't give a damn what you do for a living. We are looking for the two guys you call Allen and Keith, or Crazy A and his boy. Now where the fuck are they!"

"I don't know where those guys are, man; I don't fuck with them like that. I told numb-nuts over there not to fuck with them."

"Well, we need something to help us find these guys in a hurry, before they kill again. Do you want someone else to get killed? Shun, you need to think, and I mean think real hard, because we're not leaving here until you tell us something. Now what's it going to be?"

"Damn, man, I heard they go to this after-hours club just south of 127th Street near Michigan. I heard they like to fuck with strippers and get high in the back of the club. I don't know for sure, but I know the guy who owns the place. His name is Big Mike, and I know he fucks with them."

"What do you mean when you say, 'fucks with them'?" Frenchie asked.

"I believe he sells them drugs and they do little jobs for him."

"What type of jobs?"

"Now don't get me to start lying on them, but I heard they jack cars and shit. This other guy runs a chop shop for parts, and Big Mike acts as the go-between because the guy is afraid of the duo and don't trust them. You see, Big Mike ain't afraid of them. He tells them what type of cars he needs, and they go get them. They disguise their faces with ski masks and use guns to jack a person. I have witnessed them change plates two or three times on a car just so they can ride slick for a couple of days. After their joy riding, then they take the cars to Big Mike and get paid. He lets them spend their money in the back with the girls, were he can watch them. If they get out of hand, Big Mike and his boys handle them. Also, if Big Mike wants somebody hurt, they go out and do that too. Sometimes they go too far, and that pisses Mike off, and he won't pay them."

"Does Big Mike know what they do on their own?"

"I'm sure he does, but as long as he's getting paid, he doesn't give a fuck."

"How do we get in touch with this Big Mike?" Frenchie asked.

Shun told them he didn't have a number for him, but said they could catch him at his club that night. "He's there every night, making sure things go right both in the front and in the back with the girls."

Richie asked, "How are we supposed to know who these guys are when we see them? You are the only person we know who knows them and can point them out."

"What, and get me killed because I worked with the police! That shit right there ain't happening!"

"So how do we get inside the club, Shun?"

"*You* can't, because you look too much like the police, but girlfriend here can get in all day and night. All she has to do is dress the part and walk right in."

Frenchie said, "You mean if I dress like a skank whore, they will let me in?"

"That's right, lady. You're their type. If you are looking for them, once they hear about the new sexy lady, trust me, they will eventually show up there."

"How often do you go to the after-hour joint?" asked Richie.

"Only when one of the guys is throwing a bachelor party or something like that."

"Are there any parties scheduled for the next couple of days?"

"Not that I know of, but tomorrow is Friday, and there's always a party on Friday night."

"Okay," said Richie, "We are on for tomorrow night. We will set up the logistics. You just answer your phone when we call you. If Frenchie has no problem getting in, you just point them out to her, and we will take it from there. They won't have a clue that you had anything to do with their arrest. About how many guys with guns will be in the club?"

"They check you at the door to make sure no one is carrying a weapon."

"How about the ladies?"

"They just look them over and check their purses to make sure they are not carrying a gun or something."

"Do they use a wand or anything like that?"

"No," answered Shun.

Walter sat there the whole time, not saying a word, and he was surprised to hear Shun give the police so much information after saying he knew nothing about them.

Detective Patterson and his partner left out the back door the same way they came in, and then Richie and Frenchie left, trailed by Walter. They all went back to the station to set up the operation. The first thing they needed to do was to meet with their sergeant and walk him through their plans. After hearing the plan, the sergeant decided they would need both watches and some help from the patrol division, because it was a huge operation. They would need to clear downtown, all the way up, the ladder. But more importantly, they would have to do all of it without tipping off reporters, who were still parked outside the station.

As they sat there discussing the logistics of their plan, Sergeant Joyner of the gang unit walked into their meeting and announced that his team had been working on some leads and were trying to find out where the guys lay their heads at night. He went on to say they had developed a CI (paid informant) who was at this very moment trying to get an address. The detectives wanted to know if they had any names for the guys other than Allen and Keith.

"No, not yet," said Sergeant Joyner, "but we're working on it. Just keeping you guys in the loop." With that, he turned and walked out the room.

After he left, each man looked at the other and said, "They are trying to get the arrest."

Walter looked puzzled. *What do they mean, they're trying to make the arrest? Isn't that the point of this whole operation?*

Later in the day, Frenchie explained to him that the gang unit worked on a point system. "If they make the arrest, their unit will get credit for it, but that's not the case for our unit. Plus, whoever makes the arrest will get a lot of TV exposure and the so-called perp walk. There also may be an award for their arrest; it depends on how they are taken into custody."

Walter nodded with understanding, and she went on to say, "You know, if we have to kick down a few doors or have to shoot them or they shoot us, we usually get some type of police award. But if we get shot, we get the second highest awarded."

"Well, now you got me a little inquisitive. What is the highest award?" Walter asked.

"The ultimate of them all is to get killed in the line of duty. That's the highest accolade anyone can receive," Frenchie shared.

"Are you fucking serious! Why would anyone want to be recognized in that way when they're dead and gone? Man, I tell you, that's some dumb shit!"

~Chapter 11~

Walter had had enough for one day and asked for permission to go back to his hotel room until the operation was over. As Walter was leaving out the rear door, still dressed in the overcoat and hat, Allen was walking in the front door of the police station. Allen walked over to the front desk and asked officer Wallace if she had a Roger Keith in the lock up.

Officer Wallace gave Allen a great big smile and said, "Let me check for you."

A few minutes later, she informed him that she did and that he had been arrested for drunk and disorderly conduct with a bond set at one hundred dollars. She added that he could go to court and probably be released on his own recognizance in the morning. Allen asked if he could pay the bond.

"Of course you can," she replied, still smiling at him. While filling out Keith's release form, she asked, "And what is your name?"

"Gregory Allen, but you can call me Greg."

"Okay, Greg, and his name is Roger Keith, right?"

For Allen and Keith, being recognized by their last names had started in high school. When the teachers had taken attendance, they'd called the last name first, and that's what people had remembered.

Greg Allen handed Officer Wallace his cell phone number and asked if he could call her sometime. Blushing and smiling at the same time, she returned the piece of paper and told him that she was in a relationship. Allen went back to his seat and waited for his friend Keith to be released. Fifteen minutes later, Roger Keith was being escorted to the front desk by the lock up keeper to sign his release paper when Sergeant Joyner and his entire gang team walked right by the two most wanted men in Chicago.

Watching from where he was sitting, Allen held his head down because he recognized their informant, who was walking out the back door with them. Looking at Officer Wallace, he said, "I hope I see you again, but of course, not like this."

Gregory Allen and Roger Keith walked right past the entire Chicagoland press corps without a word being said or any attention towards them. Taking a seat behind the wheel, Greg asked Keith, "Did you see the guy who was walking with the police?"

"No," Keith replied.

"Well, that's the nigger from 79th Street, the one who sells clothes and shit. He's working with the fucking police! We're going to kill that rat tonight!"

Eric Todd had been a registered police informant for the past two years. He was paid to give information that could be used in front of a judge by police who were seeking a search warrant. Now he was being paid to help find two men known as Allen and Keith. The police gave him a cell phone and asked that he keep it with him when he went about looking for the two suspects.

Eric requested that he be dropped off on a side street near 79th, close to Cottage Grove, and once there, he walked the neighborhood, asking people if they knew or had seen the two crazy guys. He told them that he had some money that he owed them and needed to get it to them. Going in and out of several stores and up and down 79th Street, Eric looked for Allen and Keith. The police watched from a distance, trying to stay out of sight. It was at nine pm when they told him to call it a night and that they would try again tomorrow during the day, so they could keep an eye on him. The police dropped him off around nine thirty near 87th and Blackstone.

Allen and Keith lay waiting until the informant was almost home. Then they drove up, and Keith opened fire, hitting Eric six times in the chest, killing him right in front of his house. After killing Eric, they drove off, fading into the dark night.

Just as they were heading out the office for the night, the gang officers received a phone call from one of the police officers who'd responded to the call of a man being shot dead. One of the officers on the scene had found a card tucked in the dead man's pocket; it was Officer Long's, from the gang unit with his cell and private number on it. Long asked the officer on the scene if they had a name of the person shot. The officer replied, "The identification reads Eric Todd."

Sergeant Joyner immediately called his team back to work. He needed to know how Allen and Keith had found out about the informant so quickly. After running through the facts of what had happened, their theory was that he had asked too many people on the streets and that the guys had found out about it and killed him. Someone he'd talked to must have called those guys and told them someone was asking a lot of questions about them. That was the only way they could have found out so soon. They needed to go back out and re-interview everyone Eric Todd had talked to.

Sergeant Joyner notified the homicide unit that their informant had been gunned down in front of his house and that he'd been shot because he was asking too many question about Allen and Keith. For the homicide unit, this was not just another body, but the third homicide in less than a week. They knew the press and the mayor, along with the top brass needed this to end. They needed "The Murder Police" to find these killers, and find them quick!

~Chapter 12~

The raid on the after-hours club quickly became a really big operation, and the detectives now had all the help, resources, and approval they needed to carry it out. The first plan was to go in there heavy and catch the two suspects going into the club. But, what if they missed them going in? Then they would go to Plan B, which was to have Frenchie dress the part and go in, but not alone. There would be at least three undercover female police officers with her. They also would try to get a few undercover male officers inside the party too.

Detective Patterson and Byrd volunteered to wear some of their nightlife clothes and go in with Frenchie. The two detectives talked about the nice shirts and shoes they had in their closets at home and were dying to wear to the club. Kenneth even mentioned a cap that matched his shirt. Richie reminded them how long they had been working in Area South, and that someone might recognize them that would blow up the whole operation.

They also needed Shun at the station right now. They did

not want him to come up missing when it came time to move in. They called him and asked that he meet with them right away. When he showed up, they took him into what they called protected custody, in spite of his strong protest. They wanted him alive to finger these two killers before they killed again.

Allen and Keith knew the police were looking for them and felt it was time to leave the city that night. They could not risk going home for fear the police might have found out where they lived by now. They had little or no money, and their only hope of getting a few dollars was from the only person they trusted, Big Mike. They knew he would lend them enough money to get out of the city for a while. Phoning Big Mike, they asked if he could meet with them right away. They told him to come to them because they did not know if the police were watching his place. While they were asking Big Mike for help, the detectives were setting up a surveillance team to watch his club.

Mike left to meet Allen and Keith in the parking lot on 87th and Dan Ryan. He knew they needed money, but he didn't know how much. Mike brought three thousand dollars in one hundred dollar bills with him, telling them that if they needed more, to just let him know. He also let them know that the money was going on the books and needed to be paid back. Lastly, he gave them the number of a burner he had just bought in case the police were listening.

They told him they were headed to Gary, Indiana; however, Mike suggested that they go to Maryville instead, where they wouldn't draw so much suspicion. They agreed and jumped on the expressway, headed to Maryville for a few days to watch a few shows and chill out until things cooled down.

The Area South Detective Division was gearing up for an all-out assault on the after-hours joint. They didn't want to tip off the suspects or the media. The decision was made that a high school in the Altgeld Gardens housing project would act as the command post and the staging area. It was less than two miles away from the raid location, and the police could come and go using the back roads with little or no notice by the residents. The place was perfect.

The final plans were now in place. The police would hide a number of their unmarked cars within the surrounding block of the target location. The vast majority of police personnel and equipment would be hidden behind the high school in the

Gardens.

Frenchie and Shun would sit in a location where they could see who went in and out of the club, or so they thought. This was an after-hours club. There would be no neon signs or lights advertising that they were open. Once there, the parking lot was even darker than they imagined. Frenchie notified the command post of their situation and asked if it was time to go into plan B. The go to switch plans was given close to midnight with a lot of apprehension regarding the three female officers inside an after-hours joint, that time of night.

Shun walked into the club first and was greeted by all who knew him as they asked what had brought him out on a Friday night. He replied, "I thought Big Mike was having a party."

They said, "Fool, that was last week!"

Shun knew this, but he did not want to draw any unnecessary attention to himself. Once he was in, Frenchie, dressed in a short black leather skirt with high black boots and a long black leather coat, was let in with no problem. The man at the door stared her up and down and could only say, "Damn! You fine with your tall white-looking ass!"

She turned and told him, "These are my girls from Saint

Louis who are looking for a good time."

The man took one long look and said, "You ladies are at the right place!"

Frenchie and her girls were the Belles of the ball! They were an instant hit inside the club. Guys were standing in line trying to buy them drinks. They danced and partied for two hours, hoping and ready to spring into action. They took the first round and slickly poured out the others, replacing them with water every time they went to the ladies' room. Shun would occasionally walk by and shake his head, indicating no Allen, and no Keith.

After two hours had passed, Frenchie called the command post and asked, "Now what?" She was told to get Big Mike. She went back into the club and whispered into Shun ear, "Where is Big Mike?"

"I don't see him in here tonight," said Shun.

"Go find if he's in the back room or even here."

Shun agreed to ask around. He headed to the door leading to the back room and was let in with no problems. Inside the room there was a small stage with two poles, and both were being used. The two ladies who worked the poles were completely nude and would on occasion kiss or touch each other, which drew loud whistles and cheers. During their performance, money was being thrown onto the stage. In the corners, two or three guys were getting lap dances, and one guy was having sex as he tried to shield the act with his coat. Shun watched for a while before going over to one of Big Mike's men, a guy everyone called Ness because his first name was Elliott, like Elliott Ness in the movies.

Shun told him, "I came to the club expecting a party for Big Mike, and he isn't even here."

The guy looked at Shun and said, "The party was last week, man."

Shun then asked, "Is Big Mike around at all?"

Ness shook his head and said, "No, man, he's not here. He's out taking care of some business for those two stupid motherfuckers. Them dudes done got themselves into some real trouble this time. Mike's out their trying to fix the problem as we speak."

Shun told Ness to tell Mike he stopped by. Then he walked out the door and waited in the car for Frenchie's return. Once she got inside the car, he explained what he'd been told by

Ness. Frenchie was then told by the officers at the command post to go back inside the club to get the girls and wait for further instructions.

Once inside, Frenchie told their newfound friends it was time for them to go. The guys tried everything they could to get the women to stay. They offered free drinks, food, and drugs, and one guy even offered to treat all the ladies to breakfast at the Pancake House in Calumet City.

"No," said Frenchie, "we got to go. We got to catch a bus back to Saint Louis in a couple hours, but hey, we had a great time, and I promise we will be back sooner than you think." One guy, at that point offered to personally drive them back to St Louis. "Thanks, but we have to go now," replied Frenchie, and then she and the other undercover officers shouted bye as they walked out the door.

Once everyone was out of the club, they checked in with the command post, telling them that everyone was safe and asking when they were going to put the next plan into motion. They waited to see if Big Mike showed up at closing time. But Ness, along with three other guys, closed the place down at six thirty in the morning, shutting the whole operation down.

Shun was sent home, and the surveillance team was told to follow Ness.

Ness drove east on 127th Street, which turned into 130th Street, continued east for another mile, and then drove less than two blocks past what had once been the command post that had been going to take him and his boss, Big Mike down.

The police now had its first real lead. How they handled it going forward would be crucial to the investigation. Time was of the essence.

~Chapter 13~

What the police did not understand was why their well-thought-out plan had not worked. They'd had over one hundred police officers and fifty police vehicles, including cars and vans standing by. They'd even had extra lock up personnel standing by in two nearby police stations, yet they'd made no arrests. The operation had been headed by Chief of Detectives Thomas Murphy, along with Area 2 Deputy Chief of Patrol Raymond (Ray) O'Leary. They'd both been sitting in the control center, making decisions in real time, as situations changed, as to what would be done next.

Near the end, Chief O'Leary had wanted to hit the place, carry out the raid, because this was his district, but like in the movie *Heat,* Thomas Murphy had made the call to let them walk. He wanted the two killers and, at the very least, Big Mike. And though they had none of them in tow, they did have one crucial lead for the first time in Ness.

Putting their heads together, they figured out the operation had gone south because Mike had somehow been tipped off. What they didn't know was that as the police had been getting into position, one of Big Mike's guys, who lived a few blocks from the club and who'd been walking his dog, had seen the police cars on every other block. He'd counted at least six cars with two or three police officers inside of them. Although they were in plainclothes, he knew policemen when he saw them.

As Big Mike had been leaving his meeting with Allen and Keith, the phone call had come through with the warning that the police were everywhere in unmarked cars, trying to blend in. That's when Mike had decided not to show up at the club that night and gone into to hiding to figure out what was really going on.

Mike had called Ness from a burner phone for fear that if the police raided his place, they would take everyone's phone, including Ness's, to check all outgoing and incoming calls. Mike had told Ness, who'd picked up on the first ring, that he was caught up with a lady friend and would not be in tonight. He'd given Ness permission to be acting boss for the night and to call him when he closed.

After closing, Ness called the number and talked with

Big Mike, who questioned him for ten minutes, asking if anything unusual had happened during the night. "Did anyone ask where I was?"

Ness thought for a minute and said, "We had a group of girls from St. Louis stop by. Other than that, nothing."

Mike asked Ness again, "Was anyone asking about me?"

Ness thought long and hard and said, "Oh yeah, that dope boy named Shun was asking about you."

"What did you tell him?"

Ness thought about what he had told Shun about Big Mike helping the two nuts and how that might sound to his boss. He then told Mike, "I told him you were spending time with your lady."

"What did he say then, Ness?"

"He said nothing and just left".

"Did the ladies leave with him?"

"No, they left later on."

"How much later?"

Ness could hear in Big Mike's voice that he was getting upset. "What's going on, boss?"

"Nothing," Mike responded. "Listen, Ness, I need you to

look in your rear view mirror and see if there's a car following you."

"Yeah, I see a car, but I don't know if he is following me."

"Turn around and go back to the club, now!"

"Why do I need to go back, Mike?"

"Just do the fuck as I tell you, nigger! Now!"

Ness turned the car around and headed back towards the club.

"Now look in the mirror again and tell me what the car behind you is doing."

"He kept going," Ness said. Then he paused. "No, boss, they turned around and are behind me gain."

"Okay, I need you to turn around again. This time speed up and see if they try to keep up with you."

"Yeah, boss, they are keeping up, but they are trying to stay back a little. I think they know."

Before Ness could finish his sentence, Mike told him to shut up and listen. "This number I'm calling you from is dead from now on. You will not be able to reach me on this number. You got that!"

"Yeah, boss."

"I will call you from now on. If I call you and the police are listening, the code is *Hold your horses. Did you get that, Ness? Hold your horses will let me know I need to hang up.* If they arrest you, ask for a lawyer right away and ask if you can make a phone call; that's if they allow you to make one. If they do, call Black Betty. You got her number, right?"

"Yeah, boss, I got it in my phone. Listen, Ness, they will be taking that phone from you the minute they stop you, so you need to write that number down. In fact, pull over right now and do it. Do you have a pen on you?"

"Sorry, boss, I don't." Ness could hear the frustration growing in Big Mike's voice, and he didn't know what to do about that.

"I am going to have someone call you to see if you made it home."

"Who's going to call me, Black Betty?"

"If the police arrest you, tell her you need her to call your lawyer."

"But I don't have a lawyer, boss."

"She will get you a lawyer. Just keep your damn mouth

shut! You hear me! Ask for a lawyer and keep you fucking mouth shut!"

"What did I do that I need a lawyer for, boss?"

"Stop fucking calling me 'boss'!"

"What do you want me to call you, boss? That's what we always call you."

Mike was shaking his head in disgust and frustration. The more he talked with Ness, the angrier he got. He was thinking, *This fool is going to get all of our asses locked the fuck up.* Mike tried one more time. "Ness, listen to me for the last time; if they arrest you, just ask for a lawyer and call Black Betty to get him. I know you don't have a lawyer, but I will get you a lawyer. Just keep your mouth shut. Do not talk to the police. Don't ask them for a drink of water. Just keep asking for your lawyer."

"Okay, I get it now, boss."

Hanging up the phone, Mike said to himself, *"Why do I fuck with these types of stupid brainless motherfuckers? This time next week, we will all be doing real time."* He then called Black Betty, who was half sleep and yawing as she answered the phone. "Betty," he said.

She immediately recognized Mike's voice. "Yeah, boss, what's up?"

Listen to me; this phone number is not in your name, is it?"

"No, it's one of those burners you gave me."

"It's your work phone, okay; I just wanted to make sure," said Mike. "If you get a call from Ness asking for a lawyer, ask him where he is. If he doesn't know, have him ask the police where are they located so that his lawyer knows where to go. Then call me on this number right away, and I will tell you what to do from there."

"What going on, boss?"

"Stop calling me 'boss'!"

"Well, what do you want me to call you then?"

"You sound like that stupid ass!"

Before he could say his name, Betty asked, "What stupid ass?"

"Just call me on this number, Betty. I'll tell you what to do next."

"She then asked, "What was Ness arrested for?"

Mike looked at the phone, shaking his head, thinking,

What kind of people have I surrounded myself with? "I did not say he was arrested, Betty. I said if he called and told you he was arrested, then do what I asked you to do. Did you get that!"

"Yeah, boss, I did."

Mike slammed the phone down and tried to calm himself. He knew he needed to call his lawyer right away.

~Chapter 14~

It was a little after seven am on a cool Saturday morning, a day most lawyers sleep in or usually take off. Big Mike had his lawyer's personal cell phone number, a number he'd been told to use day or night. Attorney Robert Cushman was there for him and, of course, there at his usual rate. Big Mike called him Bob. He was Jewish, which was one of the things Mike liked about him; Mike had heard about all the top lawyers in the country being Jewish. Bob was in his sixties and had been practicing law for over thirty years. He'd graduated at the top of his class at Northwestern School of Law. He specialized in drug cases and had represented some of Chicago's top drug dealers when they'd been caught red-handed. Being Cushman, most of the time, he got them off.

Big Mike knew that Bob got up every morning at six am to walk to the corner store and buy three newspapers to read before getting dressed to go to the office. He sometimes worked from home, depending on how he felt. This man, in Big Mike's eyes, was rich and powerful. He drove a big Mercedes-Benz and only wore tailor-made suits and custom shirts with his initials on the cuffs. His young assistant, Samuel, was his nephew, who had just finished law school and was waiting for his bar exam results.

Bob answered the phone, "Good morning, Mike. This is Bob. What can I do for you?"

"Good Morning, Bob. I have a problem."

"Is it a big or a little problem?"

"Huge," Mike said.

"Are the police involved yet?"

Mike thought for a moment before he answered, saying, "Yes and no."

"Then that's a yes." When Mike didn't answer, Bob went on to say, "I take it you are not in custody at this time. Am I right?"

"Yes, you are."

"Where are you, Mike?"

"I'm on the streets."

"Can you make it to my office?"

"Let's say I'll be there in about an hour."

"Okay, good. I will see you then."

An hour later, Big Mike was sitting in Bob's outer office when his phone rang. It was Black Betty. With a nervous voice, she said, "Ness just called; they have him in custody at the 111th and Cottage Grove Station, on the second floor Homicide Unit. He says, they keep asking about you. They want to know about two crazies who killed five street whores."

"He told you all of that on the phone?"

"Yeah man, he did! They want to talk to you, he said. He's been there for the last two hours, and he said that a lawyer couldn't help him or you at this point unless you turned yourself in right away. Other than that, all of you are going down for murder." She then asked, "Who did Ness kill?"

Mike said, "You know that stupid motherfucker won't kill anybody."

"Then why are the police saying he killed them bitches? And it's all over TV."

Mike thought hard and long before he told Betty, "You had better go visit your mother in Detroit for a couple days. I will call you when you can come back home without any problems."

She looked at the phone and said, "I'm telling you, Mike,

I don't want to be involved in no murder shit involving them whores."

Mike told her to stop talking, get the money he'd stashed under the floorboards, and bring it to his lawyer's office right away. "All of it?" she asked.

"Didn't your ass hear me the first time, bitch! I said all of it."

Black Betty did as she was told, putting twenty-two thousand dollars in one hundred dollar bills in a suitcase and driving straight to Bob Cushman's office.

After hanging up on Betty, Big Mike walked into Bob's office and began to tell his attorney what he knew and that he had nothing to do with those two nuts going on a killing spree. He told Bob he did not know any of the women they'd killed or the reason why they'd killed them. He admitted he knew the two men who were accused of the murder, but he had nothing to do with that part of their lives. Mike admitted that they'd done odd jobs for him.

Bob asked him, "What kind of odd jobs are we talking about here?"

Mike explained, "I worked with this guy who runs a chop shop in the south suburbs, and they would steal cars for the parts he needed. We all made a little money."

"How much are we talking about, Mike?"

"Around five hundred dollars per car, sometimes a little less."

Bob looked Mike in the eye and said, "Tell me the truth right here in my office, because if you are involved in these murders and the state can prove it, you're done. I need to know just how deep you are involved with these two guys."

Mike looked back at Bob and said, "You know me; I'm a hustler, and I sell a little dope sometimes. I make most of my money off the girls, the club, and the cars. That's what I do. I'm not a killer! I have three daughters, two here in Chicago and one back in Detroit. Her mother is sitting outside in your waiting room right now. I ain't no motherfucking killer."

"Do you know where these guys are?"

"They said they were going to one place, but they are probably not there. One other thing, the police want me to turn myself in to the homicide detectives in Area South."

"Is there anything else?"

"Yes, they are holding one of my guys, Ness, until I turn

myself in."

"What does Mr. Ness have to do with these murders?"

"Nothing. He works at the club for me. He's like a bouncer and my personal security. I pay him eight hundred dollars a week in cash. He knows absolutely nothing. Bob, I need you to get him out."

"My retainer is going to be fifteen thousand dollars if you are telling me the truth. If we have to go to court, and you know how much I hate going there, my charge will definitely go up."

"Like I said, my baby Mama Betty is sitting in your waiting room with your money."

Mike got up and walked into the waiting room to talk with Betty. A few minutes later, they both walked back into Bob's office. Betty opened the suitcase and placed five stacks on the table. Each stack contained fifty one-hundred-dollar bills. Bob turned and began opening his own personal safe. He took all three stacks without even counting them and placed them inside his safe, closing the door and spinning the combination dial to lock it.

"Okay, Mike, you have retained my services. Now let's talk about what we're going to do first. The first thing I'm going to do is visit our friends at the Area South Homicide Unit and see just what it is they have and why they need to talk to you. They need to tell me why they are holding this innocent man until you come in. It makes no sense. What is your friend's name?"

"His last name is Ness."

"Okay, it's now nine thirty am. Give me your cell number. I will call you about this matter around two pm. When I call you and tell you to come in, we will sit and talk with them. When they ask you a question, you look at me, and I'll tell you how to answer the question based on what you have told me. But if they ask you a question that we are not prepared to answer, then we are going to ask for a time out. We will then talk about how we want to answer that question. Do you understand what I'm saying to you?

Big Mike nodded his head and said, "Yeah, I got it."

~Chapter 15~

Around noon, Bob made his way to the Area South police station. When he arrived, he went directly to the front desk and identified himself as an attorney. He asked the desk officer, who just happened to be Officer Wallace, if he could speak with the detectives who were working on the murders of the five prostitutes. Officer Wallace flashed a patient smile while asking him to take a seat and telling him someone would be down to speak with him in a few minutes.

Ten minutes later, Officer Frenchie Duplassis introduced herself as one of the detectives assigned to the case. She asked Bob, "How can I help you?" He informed her that he was representing his client Roderick Michael Peterson, better known as Big Mike. She then asked him to follow her up to the office on the second floor. Once inside her office, she asked him to have a seat while she gathered the paperwork. When she returned, five detectives accompanied her. Frenchie introduced her sergeant and the four other detectives.

Detective Wright started the questioning with, "What is

your client's full name?"

"My client's name is Roderick Michael Peterson, and his date of birth is June 23, 1964. His current address of record is 1836 E. Parkway, Chicago, Illinois. He currently owns and operates Big Mike's Place near 127th and Michigan."

Armed with this new information, Detective Patterson left the room and headed straight to his computer. He found Roderick right away, along with his arrest history, which dated back ten years. Big Mike had been arrested seven times for drug-related crimes and once for unlawfully carrying a firearm. He had no convictions on his record. His driving record, according to the secretary of state, showed no driving violations in the last ten years. He'd gotten one speeding ticket fifteen years ago, but had attended a class and been given his license back. This guy was basically clean, according to his record.

Detective Patterson returned to the office and shared his findings with his fellow detectives. Bob informed the detectives that he was also representing Mr. Ness. Detective Wright informed Bob that they would like to speak with his client in person. Bob informed them that this was his reason for being there: to negotiate the terms for an arranged surrender here in the station. He was a very clever and thoughtful attorney who had been doing these types of deals for years. As part of Big Mike's surrender, Bob wanted an assistant state attorney present while the detectives were interviewing his client. He assured the detectives that his client had nothing to do with the murder of those poor women and that his client was just as much a victim as they were. He went on to say that his client had no idea why these two crazy men were killing these women.

Detective Wright asked, "So the two men worked for your client, is that right?"

"Yes, they did odd jobs for him."

"What sort of jobs are we talking about?" asked Detective Patterson.

"That is the reason why we need an assistant state attorney who has the power to grant my client immunity for the things he will be admitting to."

Detective Wright said, "Are we talking about his drug business and the after-hours joint? And how about those stolen cars? Is that what we are talking about?"

Bob looked at the officers and said, "Let's say, hypothetically, you hit all the points. Still sir, we would need the ASA to approve any such deal."

"Look here, Mr. Attorney, we do not give a shit about all that other shit your client and that moron of a friend he has sitting over there are talking about. You are wasting our time," Richie said. "We are 'The Murder Police,' and we're looking for two murderers."

Bob politely said, "Yes, I understand your situation, but I have a duty to my client to protect him."

"Okay, you have him come in."

"Do you all agree to have an ASA present during the questioning of my client?"

At that point, Richie asked for a minute to consult with his supervisor and time to contact the State Attorney's Office. Bob asked if he could step outside, because he needed to make some phone calls. "We will meet back in fifteen minutes. Everyone agree?" Bob then walked outside and phoned Big Mike, who picked up on the first ring and asked, "What's going on?"

"Listen, I'm talking to the detectives right now. They know about all of your business ventures, the dope, the girls, and the after-hours joint, including the stolen cars too. But they are not interested in any of those things. They just want the two guys responsible for those murders. Let me talk a little longer and see what happens. Stay by your phone. I'll call you back once I get a deal."

Fifteen minutes later, all three officers walked downstairs, looking for Bob. They asked him to come back up to the office, where they all took a seat.

Detective Wright turned to Bob and said, "The reality is that we don't know how much or how deep your client is involved in this case, and this is the reason why we need to talk to him. Your client knows these two guys, and we think he may even know where they are hiding. The bottom line counselor is, he needs to turn himself in, and now before someone else get hurts. You can be present during any questioning, but we make no promises beyond that."

Bob stood up and repeated his offer. "No ASA, no immunity, no interview with my client."

Bob had played his hand, and the detectives had played theirs. In the end, Big Mike had to turn himself into the police.

~Chapter 16~

Bob called Mike and gave him the bad news that he had to turn himself into Area South that day. Bob did not want the media taking pictures of his client in cuffs, so he arranged for Mike to stop and pick up a large pizza, park in the back parking lot, and bring in the pizza as if he was a delivery man. Mike agreed. A thousand thoughts were going through his head as he headed to the police station. He stopped and picked up the large pizza and delivered it like Bob had told him too. He was met at the back door by four detectives and his lawyer. He was searched inside the stairwell, out of view of the media, who were still parked outside the station. Mike was taken to a room and given his Miranda warning before being questioned.

Frenchie started the questioning off with, "What are Allen and Keith's real names?"

"Roger Keith and Gregory Allen, but people call them by their last names."

"How old are they?"

"I believe they're in their late thirties."

"Do you know if they have every been arrested?"

"Yes, they just got out about a year ago."

With that bit of information, Detective Patterson left the room and ran to his computer. In less than five minutes, he had a hit on both suspects and their pictures. Patterson ran back into the room, shouting, "We got them!"

Detective Byrd asked his team to look at Roger Keith's latest arrest, and they quickly realized he'd just been in lock up downstairs two days ago. They couldn't believe they'd had the suspect in custody. Frenchie picked up both pictures and walked them down to the front desk. She showed the pictures to Officer Wallace and asked her if she remembered seeing them before.

Wallace took one look at the pictures and said, "Yes. This one here." She pointed to Gregory Allen's picture. "He gave me his phone number."

Frenchie, with a look of amazement, asked Wallace if she still had it.

"No, I gave it back to him after letting him know that I was in a relationship." When Frenchie gave her an exhausted look while shaking her head in total disbelief, Wallace asked, "Who is he?"

"Only one of the two guys who we believe end their evenings by killing their dates."

Officer Wallace stared at Frenchie and asked, "Are these the two guys who killed those ladies and buried them in the basement?"

Frenchie nodded her head yes and said, "You see what you missed out on playing hard to get?"

When Frenchie returned to the interrogation room, Big Mike was telling the other detectives where he'd last seen Allen and Keith: in the parking lot at 87th and Dan Ryan.

"What kind of car were they driving?" asked Detective Byrd.

Mike thought for a moment and said, "I believe it was a white Buick."

"Why were you meeting with them?"

"They called me and said they had some problems with some people, but they did not say it was the police. They told me they needed a few dollars until Monday, and that was on Friday."

"How much did you give them?"

Mike stood up and said, "Let me make this clear; I

loaned them five hundred dollars. I didn't give them shit! I gave them five one hundred dollar bills with the understanding they were to pay me back."

"Why hundred-dollar bills?"

"That's how I pay. It's easy to count that way."

Just then, Bob gave Big Mike that look with a raised eyebrow. Frenchie saw the eye exchange, and she asked Mike, "Do you always pay your debts using one-hundred-dollar bills?"

Mike answered, "Yes. Like I said, it makes counting the money easy." Bob knew this could be a problem later on down the line.

Frenchie asked, "Did they tell you where they were going?"

"They said Gary, Indiana. I asked them what the fuck was in Gary. Allen said he had a girlfriend there who would let them hang out for a couple of days. That's what they said, but you know how niggers lie. They are probably in Detroit, or who knows where."

Frenchie asked, "Do you know the girlfriend's name?"

"No," replied Mike. He looked at Bob, who looked at the

detectives and asked, "Are we done here?"

"No, we need a minute," said Detective Byrd. The detectives all walked out and closed the door and began talking. About fifteen minutes later, they returned and asked Bob if they could speak with him outside for a moment. Once outside, they informed him they would be holding Big Mike and Mr. Ness for a while. Bob protested and demanded they either charge his client or release him. Detective Wright reminded him they could hold him up to forty-eight hours without charging him. Bob asked if he could have a last word in private with his client before he left. He was given all the time he needed.

Bob informed Mike that the police were going to hold him in custody for a while. Mike asked, "How long?"

Bob told him, "By law, they can hold you without charging you up to the forty-eight hours, and after that, they have to either charge you or release you." He added, "This is a good thing, in that they are not charging you. This tells me they don't have anything on you. Just keep your mouth shut."

Mike asked Bob to call Black Betty and let her know that everything was okay and he would be home shortly.

Bob said, "I will tell her the truth, that we won't know for at least forty-eight hours." Bob then told Mike he was going over to talk with Ness and reminded Mike to keep his mouth shut

~Chapter 17~

Detective Byrd motioned the detectives over to his computer. He had found that Allen Keith had a parole officer named Mark Daniels, with a phone number listed right there. A call was placed to Daniels, who informed the officers that he had an updated address for both men. It was finally the break they had been looking for. With Big Mike and Ness in holding rooms, they began planning the raid that they hoped would bring the murderers to justice.

They were going to the same address both men lived at, which was a halfway house. It was a four-flat apartment, with two on each floor. The owner had a contract with the state, which paid him directly for operating a building used to house ex-sex offenders. Probation Officer Daniels asked if they could meet the contracted owner. At the meeting, he was taken into protective custody by Area South detectives. They needed to know how many men lived in that building and where. They needed to know everything he could tell them about the men living in his building.

As the detectives learned the men's names, a direct line was set up with the Cook County Parole and Probation Office, and they were given recent photos of each ex-offender living in the apartment building along with their arrest histories. The detectives ran each man's name through both systems. They needed to know what to expect come morning when they hit the place. They needed to know how much manpower it would take to control and contain at least twenty-four ex-cons.

The calls were made, and the police were in place. This was going to be an all-out assault by the Chicago Police Department on a building located near 82th and Marquette. Again, they needed a launching area. This time, it would be the water filtration plant. Area South detectives, the gang unit, and the special operation group were all in place and ready to go.

At six fifty-five am, Sunday morning, the Chicago Police Department, with the help of the Cook County Sheriff's Office and the local FBI office, carried out the most well organized and effective raid they could have possibly imagined. Twenty-two ex-cons were taken into custody and transported to Holman's Square, a police facility for processing. Gregory Allen and Roger Keith were not amongst those arrested that morning.

While all this was happening on the South Side of Chicago, Walter was living it up in his downtown suite, courtesy of the city of Chicago. He called his girlfriend Pam, telling her he had gotten them a room at the Hyatt and to bring some clothes because they were going to be there for a couple of days. She could order room service and order drinks and movies, all on him. When she showed up and saw the policeman sitting outside his door, she asked, "What's going on?" Walter told her the officer was watching the room across the hall.

Walter and Pam ordered room service and had dinner and wine in their room. After dinner, they watched a movie and made love until two am in the morning. On the other hand, Shun took his mother to her sister's house on the West Side and told her to stay there until he called her.

~Chapter 18~

Allen and Keith arrived at the Crown Tower Hotel in Maryville, Indiana, late Friday night, just as Big Mike had suggested. With three thousand dollars burning a hole in their pockets, they were planning to kick back for a few days and have a good time until things cooled off in Chicago. They headed straight to the bar for a couple of drinks and to possibly catch a show.

In the bar, they met a group of ladies from Chicago who were in Maryville for the annual Blues Fest that was being held over the weekend. The ladies had dinner and show tickets for the two nights, and a Sunday morning brunch before leaving that evening. Allen managed to sweet talk the ladies into letting them join their party by buying drinks for the whole party. He asked them what they drank, and Grey Goose was their preferred choice. Allen and Keith found a liquor store and bought two fifths. One of the bottles was for the ladies, and the other one for their suite when the ladies showed up.

One of the ladies, Darlene Lewis, who just wanted to get

away from her two kids for a couple of days, was immediately attracted to Allen and his beautiful smile. She told him that he reminded her of a young Smokey Robinson, and he knew it.

He asked her, "If I bought front row seats, would you sit with me?"

"Of course," she said.

Allen told her she could sell her ticket and keep the money, that he had plenty of money. She sold her ticket to Keith, who sat with the other women during the show. After the show, they all hit the bar inside the hotel until closing time.

Allen asked Darlene if just the two of them could meet for a bite to eat, and of course, she said yes. He told her things she was longing to hear from a man. She was a hardworking mother of two, and had little or no time for romance, so when Allen started coming on to her, she was flattered. All of a sudden, she was being meticulous with both her hair and her make-up. It had to be just right for Allen because she really wanted him to like her. She knew it would be all over come Sunday night, when it was time for her to return home, but she wanted more. She wanted him to call her when they returned to Chicago and to introduce him to her friends as her new guy.

When her best friend and roommate Roslyn, asked her if Allen was married, she turned ugly and said, "Hell no!" Darlene reminded Roslyn that she was not that kind of woman. She admitted that she really liked Allen, but it was not her style to meet a guy and go to bed with him in two days.

Allen, though, had other plans for what was going to happen in the next two days. Keith had bought some black duct tape, and their plan was to maybe get her drunk and then share her by force and leave her, like they had done so many times in the past.

When Allen and Darlene met alone for drinks, she ordered a club soda. She told him that she did not drink or smoke and had never done drugs. She wanted to talk about her two wonderful kids that she had left home and how much she missed them even after being only one day away from them. She talked about how she had married her high school sweetheart and had kids with him. She shared how, one day he'd up and decided that he no longer wanted to be married and left. She talked about how slow he was in making his child support payments.

Then, out of nowhere, the light turned on, and Allen

found this woman to be a decent person. He no longer wanted to kill her. She was not like the other women, who would sell their bodies for drugs. This woman worked a job and supported herself and her two children. He knew Keith would have a problem with him taking a liking to this woman. Keith really wanted to have sex with Darlene and then kill her, like they had done so many times in the past. He talked openly about fucking her and her roommate until he found out Allen really liked her.

Allen went along with Keith's plan to rape and kill Darlene and her roommate. They even talked about what they were going to do with their dead bodies. Allen suggested they leave them in the hotel's hall closet and hope they would not be discovered until he and Keith had left the state. Keith suggested they steal a car and leave them in the trunk of the car. "Just think," he said, "how stupid the police will look after finding a stolen car and returning it to its owner, only for them to discover two bodies in their trunk." They laughed and joked about it until late that night.

Keith asked Allen, "How is it going with her? Do you think you can get her to come back to our room?" He knew that once she was in their room, it was game on. While Allen and

Keith were planning the murder, the only question was, "Do we just kill Darlene, or do we do both of them?"

During the Saturday night show, Allen asked Darlene to dump her friends and meet him outside the bar. She told him she had made plans to hang out with her girlfriends in the bar after the show. She knew that they would not be hanging out late, because they had to pack and get ready to leave in the morning. She agreed to meet him after they went to their rooms for the night. Allen, while looking into her eyes, told her he really enjoyed talking with her and that this was maybe their last night together.

Darlene left her room at one thirty in the morning to meet Allen, against the words of her best friend. She met him downstairs in the hotel lobby. He tried to get her to come to his room, but she knew better and told him no. He then tried to kiss her. She moved her face while telling him it was too soon for her to be kissing him on the mouth. He asked if she would come to his room and get him when she was ready for brunch in the morning. She told him she would call him.

When Allen told Keith how she felt about coming to their room, Keith wanted to go to their room and force Darlene and

147

her roommate to have sex and then leave their dead bodies in the room for the maids to find the next day. Allen was still having second thoughts about killing Darlene, because he really liked her. He asked Keith to wait until the next morning. He said they would go to the ladies' room before brunch, and force their way in. After killing them, they would leave town and head to Gary, Indiana.

~Chapter 19~

The next morning, they found themselves knocking on the door of an empty room. The girls had gone to brunch earlier than they had planned. Allen and Keith went to the brunch and found the women's group sitting together and having a good time. They told Allen and Keith they'd really enjoyed the men's company over the last two days and were all packed and ready to go back to Chicago. Darlene took Allen aside and told him she really enjoyed meeting him and looked forward to hearing from him real soon. She made him promise her he was going to call her. The ladies, one by one, walked out of the restaurant, got onto their bus, and then they headed home. Darlene would never know that the ladies had saved her life by being so hungry that they couldn't wait any longer to eat.

It was now the Sunday evening after the raid, which had not produced what the police had hoped for. It was now time to go to the media and ask for their help in finding Gregory Allen and Roger Keith. The police posted the suspects' pictures on every TV station and channel in the Chicagoland area. They were also featured on the front page of Monday mornings' newspaper. "The Murder Police," held a news conference showing the suspects' pictures and calling them "persons of interest who should be considered armed and dangerous." They had set up a hotline to take tips, and boy did the leads start coming in.

Allen and Keith were getting gas Monday morning when they saw the newspaper with their pictures on the front page. They had stolen a different car out of the parking lot of the hotel and were now driving a Ford Taurus. They tried to call the number Big Mike had given them, but it kept going straight to his voicemail. Something was wrong, and they did not know what to do. They decided to go back to Chicago, because it was the only place they knew. They tried calling Ness, and it also went to voicemail.

Allen looked at Keith and said, "They must all be in jail." He then added, "We have to go back to Chicago, because I want to get Darlene."

Monday afternoon, Bob Cushman was walking his client out the front door of the Area South police station. The forty-eight hours were up, and because the police had nothing on Big

Mike, they'd had to release him. Mr. Ness had been released the day before without being charged too.

Once Big Mike was all alone in his car, the first call he made was to Black Betty to let her know he was out of jail. He asked her to remain in Detroit until the two nuts had been arrested or killed by the police. After hanging up, he called Allen on the burner he had given them. When Allen heard his voice, he felt a sense of relief. Big Mike was on their side after all. He asked Big Mike where had he been, because they had been calling him for two days and it kept going to his voice message.

Big Mike told Allen he'd been held in a little room at the police station for the last two days and the police had questioned him about his relationship with them. He told Allen he had played the nut-roll and given the police nothing over the past two days before his lawyer had gotten him released. He said the city of Chicago and its police department had an all-out manhunt in place, including a hotline for tips, with a reward for the help in the capture of them, dead or alive. He explained that while he'd been sitting in the police station, he'd witnessed over fifty detectives going over leads, bringing in folks off the street, and looking at any kind of information that would lead to Allen and Keith's arrest. Big Mike told Allen they needed to get out of town, like yesterday. He also told him not to worry about the money he owed and to never mention his name to the police if he and Keith were captured. Lastly, Big Mike said, "Never contact me again."

Allen and Keith called a few friends, but everyone they contacted told them they were too hot to be around and not to call back. Keith asked Allen, "Is there a reward offered for us?"

"I really don't know," Allen said.

They found and old boarded-up house and stayed there for the next two days, only leaving at night to get food and drinks.

Darlene had called the hotline and left her name and number. On Monday morning, she had read all the newspaper stories about the killings and could not believe she had just spent the last few nights with two serial killers, whom the papers now referred as "psychopathic killers." Her phone rang, and on the other line was Detective Felicia Duplassis.

Frenchie asked Darlene, "Did you call about the killers?"

Darlene could only say, "Yes, I did," before she broke

down crying. She tried to tell her story, but was too emotional.

Frenchie asked her, "Where are you?"

Darlene could barely give her address of 8710 Wonderland.

"Where is that?" Frenchie asked.

"One block from California. First-floor unit."

Thirty minutes later, Frenchie and Richie were ringing Darlene's doorbell. She looked out of her window and saw Frenchie standing tall in her designer coat and black beret. Behind her stood Richie, who was displaying his badge and I.D. Darlene opened her door halfway as Frenchie and Richie identified themselves as homicide detectives. Darlene opened her door wider and invited them in. She began telling her story about meeting Allen and Keith in Maryville during the Blues Fest. She and Frenchie talked for over an hour as they went into details about the weekend.

Frenchie asked, "Do you think Allen might try to call you?"

"I hope not," Darlene responded.

Frenchie convinced her to take his call, and try to get him to come over by telling him that she didn't believe what she'd read or heard about him. "Tell him you still care, and want to be with him. Did you tell him about your family?"

"No, we talked about my little girls only."

"That's good, Darlene. If he calls you, tell him your brother is a good lawyer and he might be able to help him, rather than use a public defender. One last question," Frenchie said, "does he know where you live?"

"Yes, I told him where I lived when he asked for my name and number."

"This could be a problem. Now we have to put a team on your house just in case he tries to contact you or come by."

As Darlene broke down at the news, Frenchie told her not to be afraid, that there would be police officers with her until Allen and Keith were caught.

~Chapter 20~

Wednesday, two days after hiding out in the abandon house, Allen called Darlene at two in the afternoon. He asked her to let him explain what was really going on. First, he said he was not a killer. He told her that Keith was his cousin and he was sick in the head and Allen was only trying to help him. As he kept talking, Darlene hit the red button next to her phone that had been set up to notify the police if Allen was on the phone. The police technicians began to triangulate his position. Darlene had been told that if he called her, she needed to try and keep him on the phone as long as she could.

Richie and Frenchie were notified that contact had been made with the fugitives and that the team was trying to pinpoint their location. Very quickly, they determined that Allen and Keith were in route to Darlene's house. Was this the moment they had been waiting for? Were Allen and his partner in crime about to be caught? Frenchie called Eugene and Kenneth, and they too were in route. A precise location was made. The two men were near 87th and Ashland, five minutes from Darlene's house. But they were at least twenty-five minutes away. Eugene and his partner were even further away. Frenchie and Richie were not worried because they had an unmarked car sitting a block away from Darlene's house that could see anyone who approached from the front. They also had what appeared to be a broken-down van in the alley, which doubled as a surveillance vehicle. There were two detectives sitting in each, and all were willing and ready to spring into action. This time, "The Murder Team" was ready! No more slip-ups.

Both teams were put on alert, and the task force of twenty detectives that had been put together by Area South, was now closing in too. The Murder Team knew Darlene was their only real lead and had decided to put their manpower close to her. Richie asked the task force team to switch over to zone five on their radios. Zone five was all theirs; no other unit would be using this frequency. They could talk to each other without any interference. Once everyone had switched over, Richie asked that they wait for the surveillance team to tell them when to close in.

Frenchie called Darlene on the cell phone that had been provided to her. Frenchie and Richie could hear the conversation with Allen in real time, but she wanted Darlene to say something like, "You can stay here at my house for a few days if you need to," to say, "I miss you," and even tell him it was okay for Keith to stay there too.

Darlene relayed every word Frenchie had given her, but Allen wasn't buying it. He kept asking her to come to him for fear that the police were sitting in her house, waiting for him and Keith to show up. Just like the police had a plan, Allen and Keith also had one. Keith did not trust Darlene and wanted no part of Allen bringing her with them. They knew the police would be looking for two men in a car. So in an effort to throw the police off, they had stolen a second car and were now trailing each other with a little distance between them. Allen had purchased two wigs, two coats, and eyeglasses that would normally be worn by someone elderly. They appeared to the normal passerby, to be little old ladies probably on their way to church.

Allen called Keith on his burner phone and reminded him of what Big Mike had said. It was time to get out of town. Keith was ready and told Allen, "Let's go, now!"

"But what about Darlene?" Allen couldn't explain to

Keith why he wanted Darlene so bad; he just did.

Keith pleaded with Allen to let her go. He tried to convince him they would come back later when things cooled down and get her. This was a bad time to have her with them, he expressed. Allen knew there would be no next time. The time was now! He told Keith to leave without him because he was going to get Darlene and would meet up with him later.

Keith said, "I'm not leaving without you, man." He then told Allen to pull over so they could talk about his wanting to pick Darlene up. Keith started the conversation with, "You know the police could be waiting there on us to show up, and out of nowhere, they will jump out and start shooting with no questions asked." Keith looked around and saw a lady putting her small child in the back seat of her car. He said, "I got an idea. Why don't we grab the lady and the child, and then I'll tell you what we are going to do."

Allen jumped into his car and drove up next to the lady, who looked surprised when he got closer to her. Seeing what she thought was an old lady who was a terrible driver, the lady continued opening the driver's door. Just then, Keith, out of nowhere, pushed her into her car at gunpoint and ordered her to get on the floor. She pleaded for them not to hurt her or her baby. Keith then got behind the wheel and pulled the car out while telling her that if she did what they told her to do, she and her baby would live to see another day. If not, then today would be her and her baby's last day on earth.

She recognized the men from the newspapers as the wanted killers. She said, "I'll do anything you ask, just please don't hurt my baby."

Keith's plan was now in full effect. He told Allen to get down in the back seat with the baby and let their hostage drive up to Darlene's house. "Now, if the police are there, they can't shoot us because of the baby. I will follow a short distance behind you, and if everything goes as planned, we'll let her and the baby go, and you will have your Darlene

~Chapter 21~

Frenchie and Richie could hear Allen and Darlene's conversation. They were only five minutes away. Allen told Darlene that a blue BMW with a woman driving with a baby in the back seat would be pulling up to her house in the next few minutes. She was told she should come out and get in the front seat with the lady.

Darlene asked Allen, "Where are you?"

"I'm in the back with the baby, on the floor."

"Who is this lady, and why does she have a baby with her?"

Frenchie and Richie were almost there. Eugene Patterson and his partner Kenneth Byrd were not far behind either, and they listened along with everybody else on the task force. Now, the situation had changed. Frenchie called Darlene and told her not to leave the house, no matter what!

Darlene asked Allen, "You are not going to hurt the baby, are you?" All she could think about was if it had been her two kids sitting in the back of a car with a killer. She would want another mother to do what she was about to do. Within a few minutes, a blue BMW pulled up in front of her house and blew the horn. Frenchie was back on the phone with Darlene, telling her to wait. Allen was now calling her on the phone too, telling her that he was out front and it was time to go. As Darlene looked out her window, she spotted the car, but to her dismay, she saw a young girl behind the wheel crying while looking back at her baby.

Frenchie and Richie could now see the car parked in front of Darlene's house, with the lady behind the wheel. Though they had more than twenty-five detectives in the area ready to jump into action, they had no contingency plan that involved an innocent mother and her child. Richie said to the others, "We need more time."

Allen told Darlene to come out of the house right now or something was going to happen to the baby. Upon hearing the mother's wails, Darlene told Allen she would be right out. Frenchie pleaded with her to not leave her house. Darlene said, "If I don't, he's going to hurt the baby."

Frenchie got out of the car, and Richie asked her, "What are you going to do?"

"I don't know, but I have to do something."

As Frenchie walked down the street like she did not have a care in the world, she held her Colt .45 automatic near her side. As she neared the car, she saw Darlene coming out of the front door. Frenchie could see the outline of the man hiding in the back seat of the BMW. She pointed her weapon and began firing one, two, three, and then four rounds right through the window hitting Allen in the head with the second shot. She continued firing, making sure he was dead.

Richie, while running to help Frenchie, told Darlene to go back into the house. Keith, watching from his car, stopped in the middle of the street and began firing in Frenchie's direction.

Eugene and Kenneth had turned the corner in time to see Frenchie take out the guy in the back seat. Before they realized it, the car in front of them had stopped, and the driver was now out of the car, firing at Frenchie. Without hesitation, Eugene put his feet heavily on the gas and drove his car into Keith, knocking him to the ground. While still down, Keith kept firing.

Richie wanted to fire back, but because Keith was on the other side of the car, he did not have a clear shot. However, Frenchie did! She turned and continued firing while walking in his direction, hitting him two times in the chest. Keith was dead at the hands of Frenchie. Richie pulled the mother from behind the wheel while Kenneth, who'd been able to free himself from their car, took the baby out of the back seat. The baby was covered with blood, and they could not tell if it was Allen's or the baby's, but Frenchie knew she had only hit her target.

As the street filled with detectives and uniformed officers who had been assigned to the task force, they began blocking off the street, making sure both offenders were dead. Detective Byrd could find no injuries on the baby. He then handed her back to her mother, who could not stop crying while searching her baby for wounds.

Frenchie walked back to the house and was greeted by Darlene, who was also in tears. Frenchie complimented Darlene for being brave while helping them bring the killers to an end. She told her that the city of Chicago thanked her. The Chicago Police Department thanked her. And most of all, she thanked her.

It took several hours to bring the operation and case to an end. Richie Wright had a new star in his unit, one who did not want to be a star. Chicagoland TV was interrupted to bring its citizens an important news flash stating, "According to police, the two killers at large have been brought to justice. We now take you live to Area South's headquarters. Walking to the microphone is Detective Richard Wright."

The detective took the microphone and said, "I would like to first thank these officers standing here next to me, who worked around the clock to bring these deadly killers to an end tonight. Both men, rather than give up, fought a deadly gun battle with our officers and lost. Both men were killed in the exchange of gunfire in the streets. Thank God, none of our guys were injured. I want to give a special thank you to Detective Felicia Duplassis for her bravery tonight. Her display of courage went above and beyond the call of duty. Now let me bring her up here to the microphone."

Frenchie started off by thanking her teammates, saying that without them, she could not have been able to do what she'd done that night. She thanked Darlene, whom she called a hero for what she'd done at the risk of her own life by placing herself between the killers, and an innocent mother and child. She also thanked all the witnesses who'd put their lives at risk, giving up information that helped bring the men to justice. After that, she released the microphone, walked away, and headed to her desk to call Walter and let him know everything was over.

The phone rang only once when Walter picked up. Somehow, he knew it was Detective Frenchie, whom he had just watched live on TV. He thanked her and the other brave detectives that worked in Area South for their help in solving his cousin Sandra's death.

After talking with Frenchie, Walter and his girlfriend Pam left the Hyatt without even stopping by the front desk. He was not about to try and explain anything about the bill. As far as he was concerned, the city of Chicago could afford it and then some. He and Pam got in her old car and drove off, never looking back.

The next morning, Frenchie called Bob Cushman and informed him that his two clients were no longer suspects in the murders. She finished the conversation by telling Bob they'd found over a thousand dollars in one-hundred-dollar bills. "Now, what do you think about that?"

www.ingramcontent.com/pod-product-compliance
Lightning Source LLC
Chambersburg PA
CBHW060600200326
41521CB00007B/620